UNLOCK THE SECRETS OF YOUR MIND

MENTAL CHALLENGES AND VISUAL TEASERS

Written by Ian Howarth & Patrick Green

tangerine Press

Illustrated by
Robert Farnworth, Mick Gillah, Chris Lyons, Steve Noon, Tony Smith, Paul Thorley and Lynne Willey, and at Specs Art: Shantal Freeman, Gillian Hunt, Roger Jones, Don Simpson, Gerald Witcomb.

Picture credits
AOL   Andromeda Oxford Ltd
SPL   Science Photo Library
Z   Zefa Pictures

4 AOL; **4–5** Gamma Press/Frank Spooner Pictures; **6tl** AOL; **6tr** Newbury Weekly News; **6–7** Images Colour Library; **7tl** AOL; **9tr** AOL x3; **10** Bill Redic Photography; **13** Clive Brunskill/ Allsport; **14–15** Pictor International; **16** James King-Holmes/SPL; **22cr** Nicola Sutton/Life File; **22-3** Steve Etherington/ Empics; **23cr** AOL; **27** AOL; **28tr** Mary Evans Picture Library; **28bl** National Medical Slide Bank; **28br** Alex Bartel/SPL; **34** Spectrum Colour Library; **37** Argos; **38–39** Schuppe/Z; **40** AOL; **41** AOL; **42–43** Adam Hart-Davis/SPL; **44bl** New York Metropolitan Museum of Art/A.K.G. London; **44cr** Lockheed Advanced Development Company; **46l** Robert Harding Picture Library; **46br** TRIP; **47** TRIP; **48bl** Intel; **48tr** Martin Anderson; **49br** from *Perception* by R. Sekuler and R. Blake, 2nd ed., 1990/by permission of The McGraw-Hill Companies; **50** Brinbo Books; **52** Peter Craig-Cooper/Nature Photographers Ltd; **54** Z; **56cl** Nick Leggett; **56cr** Nick Leggett; **56–7** Chris Munday; **57t** K.G. Preston-Mafham/Premaphotos Wildlife; **58–9** John Sandford/SPL; **59t** Gamma Liaison/Porter Gifford/Frank Spooner Pictures; **59br** Range/Bettmann/UPI; **61** Z; **62cr** Z; **62–3** Z; **64b** A.K.G. London; **64tr** AOL x2; **66** M.C. Escher/Cordon Art, Baarn, Holland; **69cl** AOL; **69cr** AOL; **70** Simon Bruty/ Allsport; **72br** The Kobal Collection; **72–3** Rex Features/Sipa Press; **73cr** Martin Anderson; **73b** AOL.

Editor Jenny Fry
Cover design Alix Wood

Planned and produced by
Andromeda Oxford Limited
11-13 The Vineyard
Abingdon
Oxon
OX14 3PX
United Kingdom
www.andromeda.co.uk

ISBN 0-439-23473-5

Printed in Hong Kong

Contents

What Is Thinking?

Imagining, planning, calculating, understanding others, solving problems, checking if you are right—all these things are thinking.

THERE ARE MANY DIFFERENT KINDS of thinking. We may think alone or with other people, either in cooperation or in competition. We may calculate with numbers, reason with words, or imagine things as a mental picture. Quick thinking, which often includes reacting quickly, is another thinking skill. Memory is important too, because without it we can only think about the things in front of us. When cooperating, it is important to understand the other person's thinking so that we can learn from them or teach them. All these types of thinking are used in complex activities such as the mountain rescue operation shown here. And they are also required for the Brain Games below and on the following pages. When we are competing with someone, it is important to try and anticipate what our opponent is thinking, in order to avoid any traps they might set.

Brain Games

REMEMBER THE ROUTE

Look at this collection of objects (left) for 10 seconds and memorize the position of each one. Close your eyes and ask a friend to name any two objects on the edge of the picture. Can you name all the objects on the shortest route between the two? You can play this using your own objects, moving them between each turn.

FILLING KNOWLEDGE GAPS

Each shape (right) stands for a number. These add up to give the numbers down the side and along the bottom. What number does each shape stand for, and what is the missing number? Could you find it without cracking the code? Find out on the Answers pages.

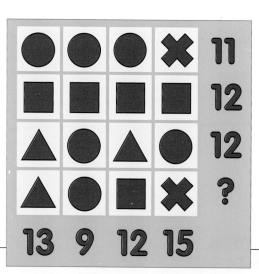

●	●	●	✖	11
■	■	■	■	12
▲	●	▲	●	12
▲	●	■	✖	?
13	9	12	15	

WHICH SWITCH?

There are three switches outside a closed door (above) and three light bulbs inside the room. How could you figure out which switch operates each light bulb, if you are only allowed to switch two of the switches on and off before going into the room? Turn to the Answers pages to find out.

WORKING AS A TEAM ▼

The leader of the team (in red) is anticipating how the victim of an accident will be rescued. He has told the assistant leader (in green) what instructions to give the volunteers, taking into account their different abilities. The navigator (in blue) is calculating distances and times on the map.

Speeds

flat ground	3 mph (4.8 kph)
> up slight hill	2 mph (3.2 kph)
>> up steep hill	1 mph (1.6 kph)
< down slight hill	4 mph (6.5 kph)
<< down steep hill	5 mph (8 kph)

15 mi (24 km)

8 mi (13 km)

12 mi (19 km)

5 mi (8 km)

g

5 mi (8 km)

j

8 mi (13 km)

f

x

5 mi (8 km)

6 mi (9.5 km)

Home

RAT IN A TRAP

This game for two people tests how quick your reactions are. Fill an old sock with sand and tie a knot in the tail to make a rat. One player drops the rat down a cardboard tube and the other has to hit it hard as it comes out (left). The "dropper" can try to make it easy or difficult for the hitter.

FIND THE QUICKEST ROUTE

A rescue team thinks the injured party is either at the red or blue flag on the map above. Which route should they take in order to reach both sites in the shortest time? The distances are marked on the map and the speeds up- and downhill are shown in the table and marked as arrows on the map. What advantage would there be in sending out two teams? (See Answers pages.)

Getting It Right and Getting It Wrong

It isn't always possible to look up the answer to a problem. Often trial and error is the only way to test if an idea will work.

TESTING A DESIGN ▲

Stability is important in a homemade raft; the design may need to be tested and improved many times.

GETTING IT RIGHT ◄

Sailboards are designed for speed. They can go faster over a 1,640-foot (500-m) timed run than any other type of craft using a sail on water; the fastest speed ever reached was 53.57 miles per hour (86.21 kph) by a trifoiler.

WHEN DEVELOPING new designs by trial and error, we are bound to have more failures than successes at first. This may not seem to be a very smart way to make improvements, but it would be even sillier to make changes to the way we do things without testing them first. The simplest tests help us avoid disasters. More intelligent tests compare different approaches. From these we can learn how to design even better ways of doing things.

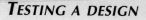

Brain Games

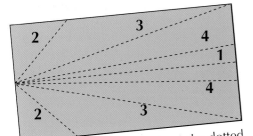

You can make surprisingly wide bridges from playing cards. In this simple one (right), there is just less than a card's length between each support. Can you design one that spans a much greater gap without using glue or tape? (See Answers pages.)

DESIGNING PAPER PLANES

Below are the designs for the fighter (swept-back wings) and the glider (long, thin wings) shown above. Try them out, then design your own planes.

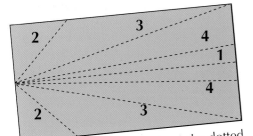

Fighter: Fold the paper along the dotted lines. Fold 1, 2, and 3 inward and fold 4 outward. Swept-back wings are fast and easier to control than thin wings.

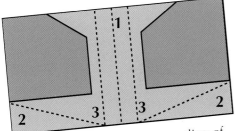

Glider. Step one: Draw the outline of the glider (above) on a piece of paper. Turn the paper over and fold 1 and 2 inward along the dotted lines.

Step two: Cut out the shaded area and fold 3 outward. Thin-winged planes stay up longer, but are hard to control. Attaching paper clips to the nose will help.

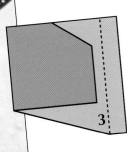

DESIGN A SPINNER

The design of a paper helicopter is not as obvious as a paper glider. But "spinners" can stay up just as long as paper planes. All you need is a sheet of thin cardboard, a pencil, a ruler, scissors, and a paper clip to use as a weight (below and right). Hint: think of a helicopter often seen in nature! See if you can design your own before turning to the Answers pages for one design.

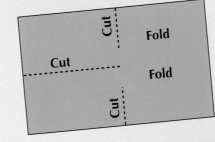

A CODING DEVICE

The disk on the right can be used for both coding and decoding messages. Write a message in code by finding each letter on the outer ring and replacing it with the corresponding letter on the inner ring. To decode, reverse the process. Anyone with the same disk can decode your messages. Or you can design your own disk. How could you make it more difficult for someone without the disk to decode the message, but still easy for someone with the disk? (See the Answers pages.)

What Are Brains For?

Some parts of our brains take in information, and other parts process the information received.

PROBABLY THE FIVE MOST IMPORTANT functions of the brain are: sensing the environment, communication, recognition, instructing the body to move, and thinking or reasoning. (Each Brain Game on the next page falls into one of these categories.) We know from recordings made of activity in the brain that the five senses—vision, hearing, smell, taste, and touch—all send messages to different parts of the brain. Other parts are involved in coordinating movement. And other parts still are more specialized, such as the area necessary for understanding speech and the area used in producing speech. Large parts of the brain have no distinct function, but may be involved in many different kinds of thinking, causing bursts of electrical energy to surge through the brain. Scientists have also learned a lot about how the brain works by studying the loss of brain function after accidents or strokes.

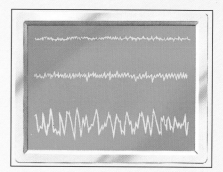

BRAIN WAVES ▲

The amount of electrical activity in your brain—recorded as "brain waves"—gives a rough indication of the speed of your thinking. When you think hard, they are fast and irregular (top row). They slow down as you get drowsy (middle row), and are long and slow when you are asleep (bottom row).

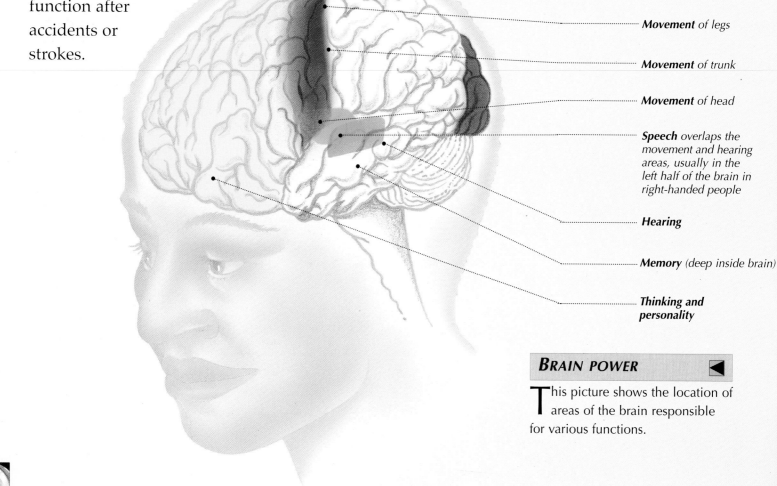

Movement of legs

Movement of trunk

Movement of head

Speech overlaps the movement and hearing areas, usually in the left half of the brain in right-handed people

Hearing

Memory (deep inside brain)

Thinking and personality

BRAIN POWER ◄

This picture shows the location of areas of the brain responsible for various functions.

Brain Games

TWO THINGS AT ONCE

Because of the way the brain is organized, some movements are easy to do by themselves but very difficult to do in combination with other movements. Can you pat your head and rub your stomach (left) at the same time? Now try locking your fingers together and rotating your thumbs in opposite directions!

SALTY, SWEET, SOUR, OR BITTER?

You can map these four main taste sensations on your tongue (right). Place a tiny bit of salt on the tip of your tongue. If you recognize a salty taste, mark a drawing of your tongue SA (for SAlty) at the tip. Now put some in the middle, then on the back and sides of your tongue, and note the result. Rinse your mouth and repeat with sugar (SWeet), lemon juice (SOur), and instant coffee granules (BItter). Compare your map with the one on the Answers pages.

WHAT IS THE MISSING CARD?

Take a deck of cards, fan them out face down, and ask a friend to pull out a card without telling you what it is. How many times do you need to look through the deck to find out which card is missing? Hint: there are only two colors and four suits in a deck, with 13 cards in each suit. Remember that **every** card has, or can be given, a numerical value. (See the Answers pages for one solution.)

RECOGNITION

Can you identify the three objects below, photographed either close-up or from an unusual angle? See the Answers pages.

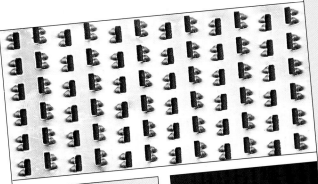

COMMUNICATION

When you draw a picture, the visual brain communicates with the part of the brain that controls movement. But can your visual brain direct a friend's movements? Sit back-to-back with a friend and describe an object to him/her without saying what it is (below). Your friend should try and draw the object. Take turns and see who is better. It is hard because the part of the brain that controls speech is not very good at dealing with visual space.

Is the Brain a Computer?

Computers do many things better than we can, and they are improving at others; but our brains still do some things better than computers.

SIMPLE COMPUTERS DO ONLY what we instruct them to, in "programmed" languages that work a little like our own. They cannot recognize faces or read messy handwriting, but they calculate much better than we can. More advanced types are being designed to be more like the human brain; they can recognize some faces and understand simple instructions given in our language. They can also learn from experience. A computer would find the two calculating Brain Games on the next page easier than you will, but you will be better at the other three! Try them and see.

COMPUTER CHESS

The first computer chess programs were easily beaten by people. But better programs are being developed all the time, and now the best ones can be beaten only by Grand Masters.

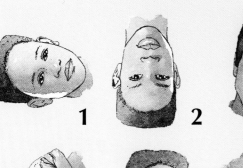

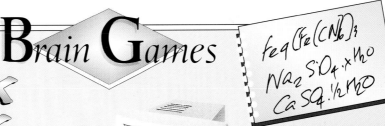

$$Feq(Fe(CN)_6)_3$$
$$Na_2SiO_4 \cdot xH_2O$$
$$CaSO_4 \cdot \tfrac{1}{2}H_2O$$

CRYPTARITHMETIC

Cryptarithmetic is arithmetic in code. What numbers do the letters above stand for, if X = 5 ? Some clever tricks can be used to solve this kind of problem, but people generally fall back on trial and error, which computers do much faster than people. (Check your answer on the Answers pages.)

READING BAD HANDWRITING

Can you read these chemical formulas (above), despite the bad handwriting? A computer can display bad handwriting on its screen, but cannot interpret the information like we can. (See Answers pages.)

1   **2**   **3**

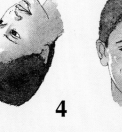

4   **5**   **6**

CRACK THE PRICE CODE

Some stores put coded prices on their merchandise (right and below). Can you crack the code and figure out the price of each of the six items? A computer could do this very quickly. (See Answers pages.)

M.NL

K.RQ
$4.96

K.RQ
$3.76

N.KK

L.ST
$3.22

L.PN

N.PL
$2.82

MATCHING FACES

Look at the faces above. They belong to three boys (there are two pictures of each boy). Can you identify which pictures are the same boy? Pair up the numbers and check your answers on the Answers pages. This kind of test is very difficult for computers.

HOW GOOD IS YOUR MEMORY?

This game is most fun played competitively. Study the objects on the tray (right) for 30 seconds and try to memorize them. Now turn away and write down as many as you can. Is your memory better than your friend's? A computer could store the list of objects in its memory until you removed it. But it could not name the objects without help.

What Will They Do Next?

Whether we're competing against someone or cooperating with them, we need to know what the other person is going to do next.

IN ALL KINDS OF SITUATIONS IN LIFE, it is very important to know what the other person is thinking so that we can predict their next move. But it isn't always easy. If someone always thinks or does the same thing, you can predict that they will do it again. But if they vary their actions, you need to look for some pattern in their behavior, or a motive behind it. In cooperative activities, such as ballet or paired figure skating, it is essential for both people to share precise information about every move they make. But in competitive games such as soccer or card games, one player may deliberately try to mislead the opponents. Team members may also send coded signals to each other, which the opposition will try and interpret so that the next move does not catch them off guard.

Brain Games

CHEAT!

Deal all the cards to three or more players (below). Player One puts one to four cards of the same kind face down and says what they are, such as one to four Queens (but he or she **can** cheat!). Player Two either puts down one to four cards immediately above or below Queens (or can also state that he or she is putting down one to four Queens), or accuses Player One of cheating. The accused player must turn over his/her cards. If he/she cheated, he/she picks up all the cards on the table. If not, the accuser picks them up. The game goes on until one player has no cards left.

WHICH BARBER?

John is on vacation in a small town in the middle of nowhere. There are only two barbers in town (above). The first shop is messy and the barber has a terrible haircut. The second shop is well kept and the barber has a neat haircut. Which barber should John go to, and why? (Look up the answer on the Answers pages at the back of the book.)

In a soccer game, the forward often tries to bluff the goalkeeper into defending a particular side of the net while kicking the ball into the other side. The goalkeeper must try to predict the forward's next move: will he/she bluff or double-bluff?

PICK-UP-STICKS

Take a handful of toothpicks or straws and let them fall in a pile on the table (below). With a friend, take turns removing one stick at a time from the pile. If you move any of the other sticks, you miss a turn. The winner is the person who picks up the most sticks.

RED AND BLUE STICKERS

Show two friends that you have one red sticker and two blue ones. Ask them to shut their eyes, then stick a blue sticker on each friend's forehead. Tell them to open their eyes (right). They should be able to figure out the color of their own sticker without taking it off, asking any questions, or looking in a mirror. How? (See Answers pages.)

GUESS THE RULE

The dealer invents a rule that the other players must figure out through trial and error (for example, any red card must be followed by a black card, or the next card played must be two higher than the last card played). The dealer writes down the rule and keeps it hidden. All the cards are dealt, and the players take turns playing a card face up (above). If their card follows the secret rule, the dealer leaves it. If it does not, it is returned to the player, who puts it in a separate pile and cannot play it again. The winner is the player with fewest cards returned.

13

Are You Right for the Job?

*Different jobs suit different kinds of people. Simple tests can show what your abilities are and what kinds of jobs might suit **you**!*

SOME PEOPLE KNOW EXACTLY WHAT THEY WANT to do when they grow up. Their "vocation" might be to work with animals, people, machines, or computers. Others find it very hard to know, partly because they have not had a chance to find out what they are really good at. To help them, all kinds of tests have been developed in the form of games, questions, and puzzles. These test a person's ability in a wide range of skills important for different jobs, such as mathematical ability, concentration, and attention to detail. Some people find details fascinating, but others are bored by them, responding better to the broad outlines of a task. How do you respond? Do you persevere until you have worked out all the details of a problem, or do you give up in despair? The Brain Games on these pages are the kinds of tests used to assess your abilities in different areas.

Brain Games

$$3 \quad \boxed{} \quad 4 \quad \boxed{} \quad 6 \quad \boxed{} \quad 5 \quad \boxed{} \quad 7 \quad = \quad 18$$

MAKING CONNECTIONS

In the electrical circuit below, there are three switches for one star-shaped light. Pressing a switch will close the open bridges and open the closed ones. Which switch, or combination of switches, must you press in order to complete the circuit via the battery and make the light go on? (See Answers pages.)

Open bridge

Closed bridge

NUMBERS GAME

These five numbers (above) give the answer 18 when one of the sets of **+** , **-** , and **x** are inserted, in sequence, into the four spaces. Is it set A, B, C, D, E, or F? (See Answers pages.)

A + - x +

B + - + x

C x - - +

D x + + -

E x - + +

F - x + +

A   B   C

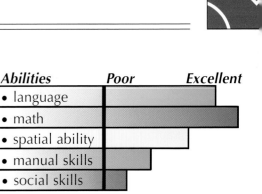

Abilities	Poor		Excellent
• language			
• math			
• spatial ability			
• manual skills			
• social skills			

ABILITY PROFILE ▲

How you respond to tests like the Brain Games below depends on your abilities in five main areas (above). Such a profile can help suggest a suitable career. This one suggests someone who might be good at computer programming.

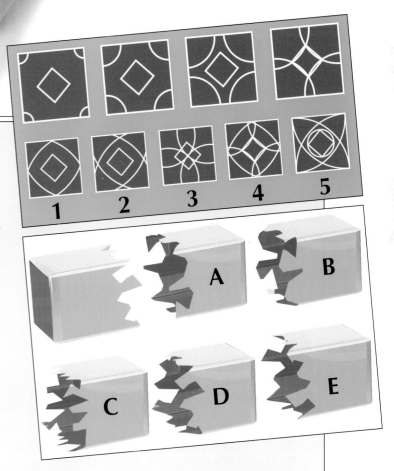

1   2   3   4   5

A   B

C   D   E

ATTENTION TO DETAIL

Many jobs require a good eye for detail. How detail-conscious are you? Write down how many little balls there are in the star, the square, the oval, and the rectangle (above). How many balls are there altogether? (See Answers pages.)

SPOT THE DIFFERENCE

Can you spot the 12 things that are different in these two pictures (left and far left)? What are they? Turn to the Answers pages to find out.

WHAT COMES NEXT?

Which of the shapes labeled 1 to 5 comes next in the sequence (top)? And which of the shapes labeled A to E completes the box (above)? See Answers pages.

Could You Be a Pilot?

Pilots must pass many tests during training. Some of these tests are like the Brain Games on the opposite page.

TRAINING A PILOT IS VERY EXPENSIVE, so air forces and commercial airlines only train the most able people. To find out who is most able, they ask the candidates to take aptitude tests—similar to these Brain Games— which are designed to help select the people with the right skills for being a pilot. The tests show whether candidates have the kinds of skills needed for flying an aircraft. These include following complex instructions, ignoring distractions, being able to keep calm in emergencies, and handling the controls accurately.

At the beginning of training, even the best trainees can make mistakes. So to avoid accidents, much of the early training takes place in computer-operated flight simulators that are just like the real thing, except that they never leave the ground.

COMPUTERIZED FLIGHT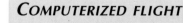

Flight simulators are like very big and very expensive computer games. You may have tried a small flight simulator on a home computer, but the professional flight simulators used in training pilots give almost all-around vision, and the cockpit can move up and down and roll around to re-create the sensation of flying a real plane. Strapped into their seats, the trainee pilots learn to move the controls accurately and make quick decisions in safety; and if there is a crash in the simulator, thankfully no one gets hurt.

B<small>rain</small> G<small>ames</small>

A<small>GILE EYES</small>

Trace this ring of circles (right). Move a pen from the top circle to the circle one place to the right. Then move two places right, by-passing one circle, then three places right, by-passing two circles, and so on, by-passing one more circle each move. Compete with a friend to see who can make the most moves in 10 seconds.

H<small>IDDEN TRIANGLES</small>

Pilots sometimes have to spot objects on the ground that are not easy to see. How many triangles can you see in this picture (left)? There are probably more than you think! (See Answers pages.)

S<small>IDEWAYS GLANCE</small>

A pilot must be able to recognize landmarks from unusual angles. To an untrained eye, this can be hard. What does the shape above look like? Check by rotating the book 90 degrees clockwise.

E<small>YE-MAZING</small>

Trace this maze (below) onto paper. Use a pencil to follow a path through the maze without touching the sides. Time yourself and count how many times your pencil touches the sides of the maze. It should take about 10 seconds. Touching the sides less than four times shows good coordination.

1 2 3 4 5 6

7 8 9 10 11 12

13 14 15 16 17 18

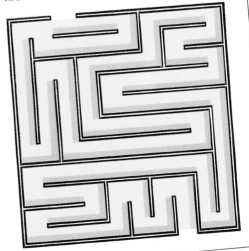

L<small>EFT, RIGHT, LEFT?</small>

Each of these men (above) is holding a bat in one hand. You must decide whether the bat is in the left or the right hand. Write the numbers 1 to 18 on a sheet of paper. Against the number representing each figure, put a letter "L" for those holding the bat in the left hand, and a letter "R" for those holding it in the right hand. Time yourself to see how long it takes. Look at the Answers pages to see if you made any mistakes. Finishing the task in 20 seconds with fewer than three mistakes is good.

How Quickly Can You Think?

Quick thinking and fast reactions are important in many sports and in some jobs, such as flying jet planes.

ARE YOU A FAST OR SLOW THINKER? It depends on what kind of person you are, on how much practice you have had, and on whether you can find clever ways to simplify your thinking. It also depends on the difficulty of the task you are performing (although this affects everyone almost equally), the time of day, your mood, how hungry you are, and whether you've had enough sleep. The Brain Games opposite test not only your ability to think quickly, but also your power of concentration and the speed of your hand-eye coordination. Compare your speeds with those of your friends, or try to get faster with practice and by using clever thinking tricks.

Brain Games

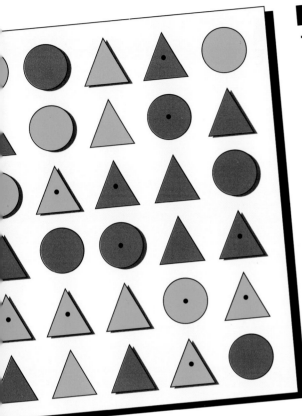

QUICK SORTING

The more types of thing you have to think about, the slower your reactions become. Count the number of objects on the left. How long does it take? Now count how many red and how many green shapes there are (i.e., two different types of object). This takes longer. Now count how many red triangles, green triangles, red circles, and green circles there are (four different types). This takes even longer. Count how many of each of the four types have dots (8 different types), then find out how many of these have shadows (16 different types). The more types of thing you have to count, the longer it takes, although each time you only consider 30 objects altogether. (Correct counts are given on the Answers pages, and a suggestion to make counting easier.)

COUNTING-BACKWARDS RACE

Distractions slow down your thinking. Practice makes it faster. Count backwards in threes from 100 (97, 94, 91. . .) down to 10. It will take about a minute (left). But with practice you can do it in less than 30 seconds. Challenge a friend to a race. Because you have practiced you will probably win easily, even if your friend tries to distract you!

STOP THE RULER!

Measure your fastest reactions. Ask a friend to press a ruler vertically against a wall. Hold your hand near the bottom of the ruler about half an inch from the wall. When the friend drops the ruler, stop it by pushing it against the wall. The faster you react, the smaller the distance it will fall. To measure your speed, trace the scale on page 75 and stick it to the ruler, then line up the zero with a mark on the wall.

HIT THE TARGETS AS FAST AS YOU CAN!

The more accurate your hand-eye coordination has to be, the slower you become. Trace the four bull's-eyes (below) onto paper, keeping the same distances between them. Move a pencil as fast as possible back and forth between the two large ones. Time yourself making 50 moves. Repeat the exercise with the two smaller bull's-eyes. How much longer does it take?

19

Boys and Girls

Do you think boys and girls are naturally good at doing different things? Or do you think it is just a matter of practice?

BOYS AND GIRLS TEND TO HAVE different interests, abilities, and ambitions. Girls often seem to be a little better with words and with people, boys with numbers, objects, and spatial relationships. Girls are also thought to be a little better at schoolwork, possibly because they tend to behave better. But tests show that differences in ability between boys and girls are in fact very small, and any differences there are may be entirely due to different interests and experiences. The difference in ability between boys and girls is much less than the range of ability within each sex. The Brain Games on these two pages are the kind that boys might find easier than girls. Test this out with your brothers and sisters!

You can also find out things about your personality by examining your immediate reaction to these games. Strong-willed or stubborn people—both girls and boys—tend to practice the things they find difficult until they become good at them. But most of us spend more time doing things we are already good at.

Brain Games

TURNING THE COGS

Here are three sets of cogwheels (below). If you turn the first cogs in the direction of the arrows, will the two buckets on A go up or down, and will the last cogs of B and C turn clockwise or counterclockwise? Write down your answers and check them on the Answers pages.

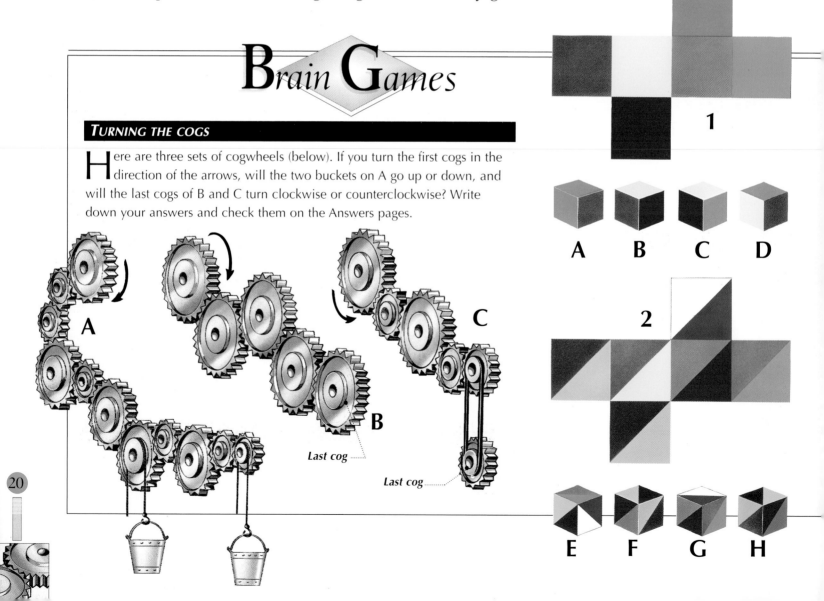

A

B

C

Last cog

Last cog

1

A   B   C   D

2

E   F   G   H

SPELLING TEST

What is the 11-letter word that all college graduates spell incorrectly? Try this one on your friends before turning to the Answers pages!

MAKING BOXES

Which box—A, B, C, or D (top left)—can you make from cardboard cutout number 1, and which box—E, F, G, or H (left)—from cardboard cutout number 2? (Answers on the Answers pages.)

NEXT IN THE SEQUENCE

Look at the two sets of eight shapes above. In each set, the pattern of shapes changes in such a way that you should be able to figure out the missing ninth shape. For each set, is it box A, B, C, D, E, F, G, or H? (See Answers pages.)

A B C D

E F G H

A B C D

E F G H

Does Practice Make Perfect?

It usually does, but it has to be the right kind of practice.

NO MATTER HOW smart you are, you can't become an expert at something like chess or playing a musical instrument without lots of practice. It takes years of practice to become world class, and the brain needs practice as well as the body. It is usually impossible to practice all of a complicated skill when you start, so you must practice parts of it separately, progressing to the complete task as you improve. But what sort of practicing should you do? Imagining doing the task without actually doing it is a surprisingly good form of practice; it helps you avoid mistakes when you do perform the task. Try the Brain Games here and see what kinds of practice help you get better.

HIGH-SPEED THINKING ▼

Even sports superstars as skillful as Formula One racing drivers need to practice, and special sessions are set up for this before each race. Racing drivers often play sports such as tennis, because being fit helps them improve their racing skills.

KEEPING IT ALL IN THE AIR

Juggling is a case of "practice makes perfect." Here's how to do it.

Step one: Start with one ball. Toss it up in the air from the right hand to the left hand, then pass it quickly back to your right hand and repeat until you can do both things rapidly.

Step two: Next, start with one ball in each hand and while throwing the one in the right hand over to the left hand, pass the one in the left hand to the right hand and continue.

Step three: Now start with one ball in the right hand and two in the left. If you throw the one in the right hand high enough, you will be able to move both of those in the left hand into the right hand one after the other, tossing the first into the air before passing the second across. It usually helps to imagine doing it with the extra ball before trying it for real.

Brain Games

CHINESE WRITING

It takes a lot of practice to learn a new language. Chinese is especially hard because Chinese writing is made up of pictures called characters instead of letters. Each of the lines on the right contains the characters for mountain, moon, and heart. Can you pick them all out? (See Answers pages.) Practice copying the characters using a paintbrush and thin black paint. Do you get faster with practice?

山 mountain

月 moon

心 heart

金 望 秫 念 哪
耻 有 意 固 朦
发 閟 服 屺 愛

A

B

MAKE A CIRCLE IN THREE MOVES

Change shape A to shape B (above) by moving only three of the marbles—or you can use coins. The moved marbles must not be picked up, and they must stay close to at least two others after each move. Check your moves on the Answers pages. You may find it difficult even then!

MIRROR MAZE

Draw a maze like the one above (or copy the one on page 17), and put it behind a screen or book so that you cannot see it. Then put a mirror beyond the maze so that you can see its reflection. Follow the path through the maze by looking in the mirror. You will improve rapidly with practice!

Is It Just a Trick?

Sometimes the solution to a puzzle—reached by careful thinking—can look like magic!

THINKING ABOUT WHAT HAPPENS to things when they are turned, bent, or stretched is called topology. It can lead to many surprising effects that look like tricks until you begin to think about shapes more clearly. A T-shirt only has four holes, no matter how you twist and turn it; a coat only has three holes; and a sock only one. We can do surprising things with our clothes, and with other shapes, when we bend and stretch them. For example, it is possible to take off a vest without taking off your jacket, even though when you try, the two garments appear to be linked together.

3

2

1

Brain Games

KNIGHT MOVES

Can you make the two red knights and the two yellow knights on this miniature chessboard (below) change places using only "legal" knight moves? The legal moves are shown by the white lines. You must stay within the squares on the chessboard shown here. Only one piece at a time is allowed on any square. You might want to practice with real chess pieces and a real chessboard. (See Answers pages.)

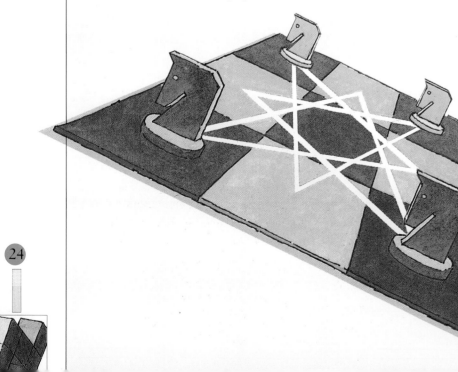

MATCH THE ROTATED SHAPES

Two of the shapes below have been rotated so that you see them from a different angle. Can you pair up the corresponding shapes? Two of the shapes cannot be paired up. Which two are they? (Check your answers on the Answers pages.)

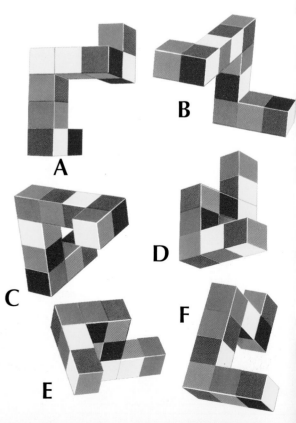

A

B

C

D

E

F

UNDRESSING INSIDE OUT ▼

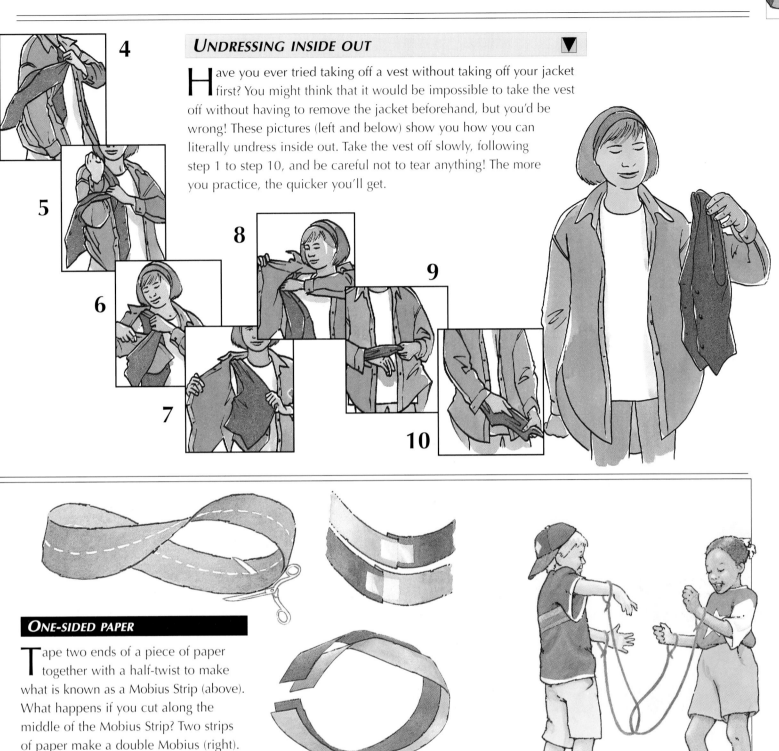

Have you ever tried taking off a vest without taking off your jacket first? You might think that it would be impossible to take the vest off without having to remove the jacket beforehand, but you'd be wrong! These pictures (left and below) show you how you can literally undress inside out. Take the vest off slowly, following step 1 to step 10, and be careful not to tear anything! The more you practice, the quicker you'll get.

ONE-SIDED PAPER

Tape two ends of a piece of paper together with a half-twist to make what is known as a Mobius Strip (above). What happens if you cut along the middle of the Mobius Strip? Two strips of paper make a double Mobius (right). Make one and cut it in the same way. What happens? (See Answers pages.)

WHAT KNOT

The top knot (right) is a reef knot, used to tie sails on a sailboat. The linked loops make it secure. However, by threading one end through the knot, you can unlink the loops so that the knot can be untied by pulling the two ends. This is called a slipknot. Which of the knots on the right (A or B) is a slipknot? (See Answers pages.)

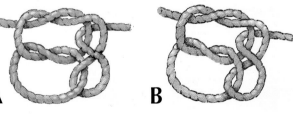

A   B

GET UN-KNOTTED

Tie yourself to a friend, as shown above. Use long loops, but do not tie them too tightly around your wrists. The two loops seem to be linked, but in fact they are not. How can you separate yourselves from each other without untying the knots? (See Answers pages.)

More Tricks

Scientific breakthroughs that challenge conventional ideas are often difficult to accept and can look like "tricks."

UNTIL THE 1600s, people thought that different types of objects moved naturally at different speeds. The Italian scientist Galileo Galilei was the first person to suspect that all things move at a constant speed until a force acts upon them. To most people at the time, this was unbelievable. Galileo claimed that, except for things like feathers, which are slowed by the resistance of the air, all objects fall at the same rate. He showed that he was right by dropping a cannon ball and a bullet from the top of the Tower of Pisa at exactly the same moment, and finding that they landed at the same time. Once people realized that force is needed to speed things up or slow them down, they began to understand things like friction and lubrication, and could measure the forces exerted by machines. The Brain Games opposite can be solved logically or by trial and error (experiments). Scientists usually make discoveries by a combination of both methods.

GALILEO'S TELESCOPE ▲

In 1609, Galileo looked at the planets through a telescope. He was one of the first people ever to do so. Like the earlier Polish astronomer Nicolaus Copernicus, he concluded that the Earth and the planets move around the sun. Because this was such a revolutionary idea and against the teaching of the Roman Catholic Church, he was eventually convicted of heresy and spent the rest of his life under house arrest.

AMAZING DISCOVERIES ◀

Galileo dropped a cannon ball and a bullet from the top of the Tower of Pisa at the same moment, and both hit the ground together. Later, the English scientist Isaac Newton suggested that the Earth was "pulling" them toward it. At first people thought this was nonsense too!

Brain Games

WHO IS THE TALLEST?

These five boys, numbered 1 to 5 (right), are each a different height. Can you figure out the names of the tallest and the shortest if: Peter is taller than Dave, Jack is taller than Alan, Dave is taller than Tom, and Alan is taller than Peter? Write down on a piece of paper the name of Number 1 and the name of Number 5, then turn to the Answers pages to see if you are right.

1   2   3   4   5

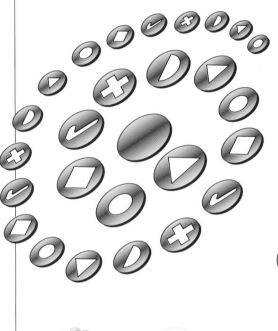

NEXT IN THE SEQUENCE

Which of the six disks labeled A to F below is next in the sequence at the center of the spiral on the left? Think carefully about the pattern of shapes before you decide. Find out on the Answers pages.

A   B   C   D   E   F

GUESS-THE-CARD GAME

Look at the 10 cards laid out below. Ignoring the suit, can you figure out what the number of the face-down card is? (Check your answer on the Answers pages.)

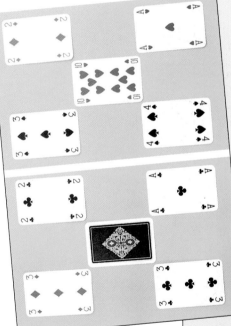

ARE YOUR WIRES CROSSED?

Connect all three utilities—water, electricity, and gas—to each of the three houses (left) without crossing any of the pipes or cables. This one may bend your mind for quite a while! (Turn to the Answers pages if you get desperate.)

THE SHEEP PEN PUZZLE

The sheep pen on the right is made of 12 panels. It is just big enough to hold six sheep. If the farmer buys six more sheep, how many more panels will he need to double the size of the sheep pen? (See Answers pages.)

The Missing Link

One piece of missing information can be all you need to solve a problem, but it isn't always easy to find.

IMPORTANT SCIENTIFIC DISCOVERIES can take scientists many years to make, or they can happen in an instant almost by accident, all because one vital piece of missing information falls into place. And even when an important discovery is made, it can be years before its significance is understood. A Scottish doctor, Alexander Fleming, spent most of his life in a laboratory looking for ways to kill bacteria, the germs that cause many infections and which can lead to death. One day in 1928, when he was experimenting with a particular bacterium, he noticed that it did not multiply near some mold that was growing on the jelly, or culture, on which he was growing the bacteria. The mold, called *Penicillium*, produced a substance that killed bacteria. About 20 years passed before other scientists extracted antibiotics from mold in order to treat infections.

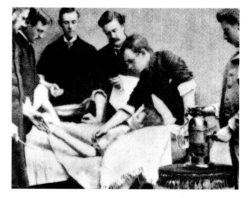

ANTISEPTIC BREAKTHROUGH ▲

Until the late 1800s, many people died after operations because nobody realized that germs cause disease. The English surgeon Joseph Lister first saw the link. He discovered that after washing his hands in carbolic acid, cuts did not get infected. Lister's antiseptic carbolic spray, used during surgery (above), saved countless lives.

Bacteria killed
by antibiotic

Bacteria unaffected
by antibiotic

ANTIBIOTICS ◄ ▼

The bluish-gray areas of mold on this loaf of bread are the fungus *Penicillium*, some species of which are used to produce the antibiotic penicillin. On the culture in the petri dish (left), the areas free of bacteria surround places where an antibiotic has been applied.

Brain Games

THE MISSING PICTURE

Trace the pieces of this jigsaw puzzle (below) onto cardboard—colored on one side only so you know which way up the pieces go—and cut them out very carefully. Now put them back together. It is much harder to do a puzzle in which shapes, rather than pictures, are the only visual clues for fitting the pieces together.

Cave   Forest   Camp   Mountain   Hill   Footprint

ISLAND MYSTERY

A mysterious footprint has been found somewhere on a desert island, but where? Make a map that shows the location of all the symbols above, using the information given here. Day one: today we went into the forest in the corner of the island NE of our shipwreck on the nearest part of the coast. The forest surrounds a cave. Day two: we have found a sandy cove on the SE of the island, and have made camp there. Day three: from our camp we can see a range of coastal mountains due west. The tallest is visible from the hill just north of our camp. Day four: we have found a footprint just north of the mountains. We are not alone! (See Answers pages to check your map.)

TESTING SINGLE SENSES

It is much more difficult to identify things just by feel or smell than by sight alone. Here is a game to test the sense of touch (right). Take apart an object such as a pepper mill and put the pieces into a bag. Blindfold a friend and ask him/her to identify the object and then put the pieces back together without taking them out of the bag. To test your powers of smell, try while blindfolded to identify flowers or food by their scent alone.

TOUCHING WITH SPOONS

Here the missing links are sight and sensitive touch. Blindfold a friend and give him/her two spoons. Then ask the friend to identify familiar objects that you put in front of him/her by "feeling" them with the spoons. It isn't easy!

Getting Stuck and Thinking Sideways

For ages people were stuck with the idea that a flying machine had to be lighter than air if it was to fly!

A PROBLEM MAY SEEM IMPOSSIBLE not because you don't know enough, but because your imagination is limited by other things you do know, or by false assumptions. But it is possible to escape such limitations just by "thinking sideways." This is called "lateral thinking." Many great inventions were thought of in this way, including the first successful flying machine. It was invented in 1903 by two American brothers, Wilbur and Orville Wright, who realized that a machine that was heavier than air could fly if only it could be made to move fast enough.

Brain Games

THE NINE TREES PROBLEM

Mary has been sent to gather apples from the orchard on her bicycle (left). With the extra weight in her basket, she finds it difficult to turn corners and prefers to move in straight lines, making as few turns as possible. After a lot of thought, she thinks of a way to visit all the trees by making only three turns on her bicycle. How does she do it? Could you do better? (The Answers pages give one solution.)

AMAZING MIND-READER

Put a handful of keys on a table (left), turn your back and ask a friend to pick one up and concentrate on it for about a minute before putting it down. Now quickly touch the keys to find out which one they chose. Tell them you have read their thoughts! How is it done? (See Answers pages.)

FLYING HIGH ▲

The world's first successful airplane, *Flyer 1*, took to the air on December 17, 1903, and flew 120 feet (36.5 m) before landing. Two propellers were mounted behind the wings to push the plane forward. The pilot lay in a cradle on the lower wing, next to the engine.

TWO TRIANGLES INTO EIGHT

These two triangles have been made using six pencils (above). Can you arrange them so that they make four triangles of any size? Easy? Now make four equal-sized triangles! Can you also make eight uneven-sized triangles? Do not look up the answer on the Answers pages until you have tried all three.

THE TEN-BALL TRIANGLE

By moving only three balls, change the triangle on the far left, with the line of four balls at the bottom, to the shape of the triangle on the left, with the line of four balls at the top. (The answer is on the Answers pages.)

TOO SHORT TO REACH

Elizabeth is trying to tie two pieces of string together, but she can't reach both of them at once (above). Suddenly she realizes how to do it. The only things she has with her are a pair of scissors, a pencil, some tape, and some glue—and the squirrel! How does she solve the problem with lateral thinking? (See the Answers pages for one solution.)

Aha! Now I've Got It!

Some problems are solved with "a flash of inspiration." Even animals have these moments of brilliance.

A NEW IDEA MAY COME TO YOU suddenly, but it does not come out of thin air. It comes because you already have all kinds of information, and suddenly you see a way to put the pieces together. "Aha!" you think. "Now I've got it!" Sultan the chimpanzee had a flash of inspiration like this when he made a tool long enough to reach some fruit outside his cage. But before he had the idea of using the tool to reach the fruit, he had already spent a lot of time playing with bamboo sticks and fitting them together for fun.

When you do the Brain Games on these two pages, you may get the same "Aha!" feeling he had.

CHICKEN-FOX-GRAIN

A farmer is on his way to market with a chicken, a fox, and a sack of grain (below). Before he reaches town, he has to cross a river, but his little rowboat is only big enough to hold himself and one other thing at a time. Chickens eat grain and foxes eat chickens! How can he transport the chicken, the fox, and the grain to the other side of the river without ever leaving the fox alone with the chicken or the chicken alone with the grain? (See Answers pages.)

SULTAN'S BRIGHT IDEA ▲

Sultan was given a stick that was long enough to reach a second stick outside his cage, but not long enough to reach a third stick or the pile of fruit a little further away. Eventually he realized that he could use the first stick to reach the second one, and by joining the two together he could reach the third stick. With all three sticks joined together, he could reach the fruit!

COINS INTO CUPS

Can you put all 11 counters—or coins—(above) into three cups so that there is an odd number of counters in each cup? Easy? Now do it again using only 10 counters. (You will groan at the answer on the Answers pages!)

TRUTHFUL AND UNTRUTHFUL TWINS

There are two twins at a fork in the road (above). One always tells the truth, the other always tells lies, but you don't know which is which. One road leads to disaster, the other to safety. You can find out which road is the safe one by asking either twin just one question. What question should you ask? (See Answers pages.)

PUZZLE DISKS

Place four disks of progressively smaller size in one of three spaces, as shown below (you could use four coins of different sizes, or cut counters out of cardboard). Moving one disk at a time, and without ever placing a larger disk on top of a smaller one, move the pile of disks—still ordered by size with the smallest one on top—into one of the other spaces. Answers pages reveal all.

Thinking Like a Scientist

Scientists solve problems in much the same way as the rest of us. But they focus on problems that no one has solved before.

A SCIENTIST DOES TWO EQUALLY important things. One is to come up with new ideas based on long-term study and research. The other is to test these ideas carefully before letting other people make use of them. The Austrian zoologist Konrad Lorenz found that chicks or goslings that he hatched in an incubator followed him as if he were their mother. He believed this was because they "imprint," or latch on to the first moving thing they see after they hatch. This idea has been tested many times by scientists. They have found that chicks will imprint on all kinds of odd things, from a shoebox to a teddy bear! The Brain Games opposite enable you to make your own scientific discoveries and then test them.

MISTAKEN FOR MOM! ▼

The first moving thing that these goslings saw when they hatched was a Dalmatian dog, so they now think that the dog is their mother! In order to survive, goslings need to distinguish their mother from other geese the moment they hatch. Human babies take much longer.

Brain Games

THE MINIMUM OF COLORS

On the left is a map of Australia and above is one of the USA (minus Alaska and Hawaii). States that share a border are colored differently for clarity. Australia can be colored with a minimum of three colors. America needs four. Can you invent a map that needs five colors? (See the Answers pages.)

SEPARATING SUBSTANCES

Valuable substances often need to be separated from other substances. How could you separate a mixture of sawdust, salt, and iron filings (above), using only water and the tools shown? (See the Answers pages.)

MAKE A PAPER WING

Can you design a simple wing that actually lifts when air flows over it, from just a sheet of paper, a pencil, and some tape or glue (above)? Think about the shape of a real wing in cross-section. Is it wider at one end than the other? Experiment with different shapes. (See one suggestion on the Answers pages.)

A DISPLACEMENT GAME

Mix two separate solutions of salt in water, making one much stronger than the other (left). How can you measure the relative amount of salt in each without separating the salt from the water? Hint: all you need is a pencil and weight. See the Answers pages.

PUTTING THE COLORS BACK INTO LIGHT

White light from the sun makes a rainbow when it shines through rain. Another way to separate the colors that make up white light is to shine a thin beam of sunlight through a prism or a glass of water. To get a beam, cut a hole in some cardboard, hold it up to a window, and close the curtains, except around the hole.

Using two prisms, you can mix the colors to get white light again. How? (See Answers pages.) If you don't have a prism, you can get a similar effect by coloring a cardboard disk with the colors of the rainbow and spinning it. Draw stripes from the center to the edge of the disk, all the way around. Twist the string and let it untwist quickly so the disk spins.

Beam of light

Are There Any Really New Ideas?

Most ideas that seem new are only new combinations of old ideas. Really new ideas are very rare, and most people never have one.

THE SCIENTIST THOMAS EDISON, who invented motion pictures, the electric light bulb, sound recording, and probably more things than anyone in history, described invention as "99 percent perspiration and 1 percent inspiration." Most of the perspiration comes from finding new uses for old ideas. People in the Stone Age learned how to cook, probably from finding charred meat or vegetables after a forest fire. Since then many new ways of cooking have been invented, but they all make use of heat. Other people may think that our ideas are original, but only because they do not know where the ideas came from. The Brain Games below all make use of ideas found elsewhere in the book.

Brain Games

FIND THE HIDDEN OBJECTS!

There are 10 hidden objects in this picture of a football game (left). Can you find the following: a flag, a large pair of glasses, a microphone, a bottle of ketchup, a large glass, a fork, the number 4, a mallet, a walking boot, and a tennis ball. (See the Answers pages.)

MOVING THE BEAD, LIKE MAGIC!

Make this simple puzzle from a piece of thick cardboard, some string, and a bead or ring (right). How can you move the bead from the loop on the right to the loop on the left without untying the string? (See the Answers pages.)

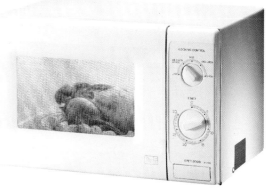

COOKING WITH HEAT ◀ ▲

Fire—the only method of cooking food in the Stone Age—emits "radiant" heat, which is absorbed by the surface of the food. By a process called conduction, it then heats the inside of the food. Modern microwave ovens send out a different form of radiant heat that penetrates deeper into the food, heating the inside directly.

CORRECT THE SUM IN NO MOVES

The sum in Roman numerals below is incorrect. How can you correct it without moving any of the pencils? (See Answers pages.)

TIE THE KNOT

Hold one end of a piece of string in each hand (right). Now tie a knot in the string without letting go of either end. Try it on your friends before turning to the Answers pages.

ODDS OR EVENS?

Throw a handful of coins (or cardboard disks, green on one side, yellow on the other) onto a table (below). Count the number of heads (or greens). If it is an odd number, ask a friend to turn over pairs of coins—either two heads or two tails (yellows) or one of each—until they get an even number. If you start with an even number, keep turning until you get an odd number. Think about the problem before turning to the Answers pages.

12-STRAW PROBLEM

Using 12 straws (left), make six equal-sided squares. You may need to think sideways if you get stuck! (Turn to the Answers pages as a last resort.)

Why See?

All five of your senses are important, but you probably depend on your sight even more than you realize.

SEEING HAS SOME SPECIAL advantages as a way of finding out about your environment. Light bouncing off the things around you reaches your eyes almost instantly, whether the things are close or far away. Unless it's foggy or very dark, you can use your sight to move around quickly and safely. Most animals that make little use of their eyes, and rely on touch and smell, have to move slowly. Seeing can be important even when you are using your other senses. Most people do not develop much sense of touch or smell, but people who lose their sight find that their other senses are full of information. Try the Brain Games below to find out how much information you can obtain without using your eyes.

FLYING BY EAR

Bats can fly swiftly and hunt for food in complete darkness. They don't need light or sight; they find their way by listening to the echoes of their own high-pitched squeaks.

Brain Games

TOUCH TEST

Test your sense of touch. Ask someone to fill some dishes with substances that have different shapes and textures (below). They should do this out of your sight, and without telling you what they are putting in the dishes. They could use pasta, cereal, candy, bread crumbs, pebbles, buttons, dry leaves, soil, twigs, or sawdust. Now, with your eyes closed, try to guess what each one contains by feeling with your fingers.

DO YOU KNOW YOUR FRUIT?

Test your senses of taste and smell. Ask someone to give you pieces of fruit (left) while your eyes are tightly closed. The different fruits should be the same texture—different kinds of berries; grapefruit, lemon, and orange; or apple and pear. Taste each one. Can you tell what they are without seeing them? You could also try this with several different flavors of soda or juice—or different kinds of cheese or chocolate. How well can you tell them apart? Does your sense of taste depend on what your eyes tell you to expect?

SWIMMING BY EAR ▼

Dolphins also have a very sharp sense of hearing, which they rely on instead of sight. They make loud squeaks that travel through the water and bounce off any objects nearby. The echoes of the squeaks tell dolphins where things are in the water around them—the fish they eat, dangerous obstacles, or other dolphins. This sense is called echolocation. Sailors in submarines use similar equipment called sonar to locate other ships and explore the ocean floor.

WHAT'S THAT SOUND?

Can you hear what's happening around you (right)? Stand in the middle of a room with your eyes shut (or blindfolded) and ask a friend to move quietly around you, stopping in different places to make noises like crumpling a piece of paper or tapping on a glass. Can you tell what your friend is doing, and where he or she is?

READING BY TOUCH

Write a message on a piece of paper (below) by resting it on a soft surface and pressing hard, so that you can feel ridges on the other side. Make the letters about an inch (2.5 cm) high, and write backwards so the message is the right way around on the other side. Now see if a friend can shut their eyes and read it by running their fingers over the raised letters!

How Your Eyes Work

Your eyes carry out the first vital step in seeing—they form an image of your surroundings.

WHEN YOU SEE something, what happens in your eyes? Light reflected from the object you see passes through the pupil, which is the dark spot in the center of your iris—the colored part of your eye. The light hits millions of cells packed together at the back of the eye (the retina). These cells act like electric switches, turning on as light hits them. They send instant messages to the brain with information about the object the eye has seen, such as its color and distance. An image of the object is formed on the retina and focused by the cornea and the lens. Your lenses adjust by becoming thicker or thinner, depending on whether you are looking at things close-up or in the distance. They become less flexible with age, so most elderly people need glasses. These Brain Games show you some of the ways your eyes work.

THE UPSIDE-DOWN IMAGE ▼

The eye's cornea and lens bend rays of light from an object to form an upside-down image of the object on the retina.

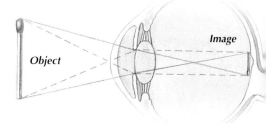

Object / Image

Pupil The opening through which light passes ....

Lens changes shape to focus image on retina ....

Cornea protects the lens and assists focusing ....

Iris controls the opening of the pupil in response to light ....

WHO SEES BEST? ▼

All animals with backbones have eyes built in the same way as humans, but seeing is much more important for the survival of some animals than it is for others.

Some small mammals, such as the shrew hedgehog, have poor eyesight. They rely on their sensitive whiskers and their sense of smell to find food.

A bird of prey's ability to pick out detail is 30 times better than ours.

Primates need good eyesight to judge distances when leaping through trees.

A civet relies more on its sharp hearing and highly developed sense of smell than on its sense of sight.

Brain Games

THE SHRINKING PUPIL

The size of your eye's pupil changes automatically depending on how much light is available (below). Cover one eye for several seconds and look in a mirror. Now uncover the eye. See how the pupil grows smaller as it reacts to the extra light coming into the eye.

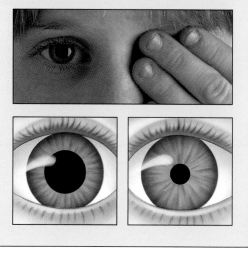

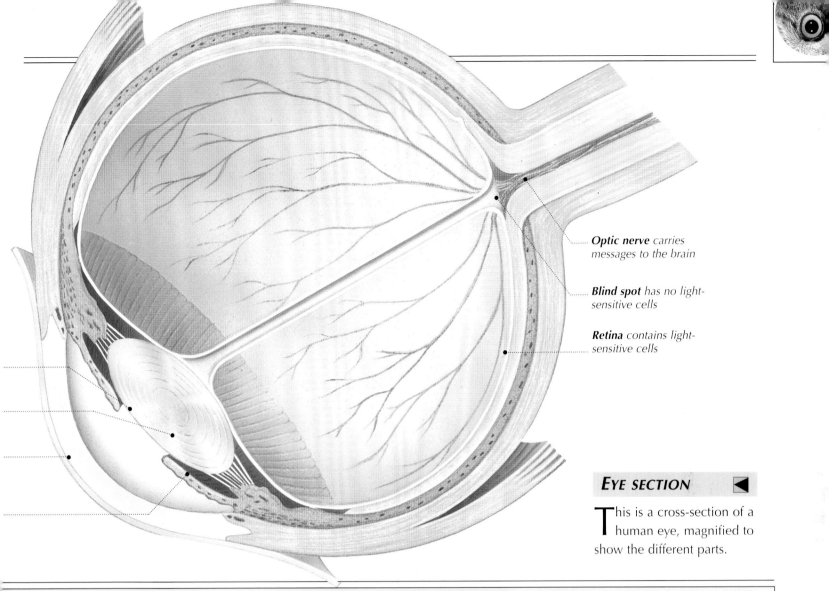

Optic nerve *carries messages to the brain*

Blind spot *has no light-sensitive cells*

Retina *contains light-sensitive cells*

EYE SECTION

This is a cross-section of a human eye, magnified to show the different parts.

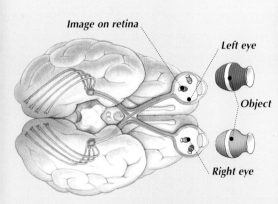

Image on retina

Left eye

Object

Right eye

BINOCULAR VISION

Since your eyes are set slightly apart, each one sees an object from a slightly different angle (left). The combination of these different views helps you judge an object's distance. Try threading a needle with one eye closed. It's hard to do because without the view from both eyes you cannot accurately judge the distance between the needle and thread.

FLOATING FINGER

Hold your index fingers about 6 inches (15 cm) in front of your eyes, with the tips nearly touching (right). Look between your fingertips and focus on the distance beyond them. You should see a disembodied finger floating in space. This happens because your brain combines the different images from your two eyes.

FIND YOUR BLIND SPOT

Close your left eye and stare at the X above with your right eye. Hold the book at arm's length and slowly move it toward you until the spot on the right disappears. This happens when light from the spot is focused on your "blind spot," where there are no light-sensitive cells.

The Adaptable Eye

In order for you to see, your eyes have to keep moving and adjusting to changing light.

YOUR EYES ARE ALWAYS adjusting so that you can see the world around you. As the light around you grows dim or becomes brighter, the pupils of your eyes expand or contract to let in more light or less, and the cells at the back of your eye automatically turn their light sensitivity up or down. You can experience this when you go from a dark room into sunlight. At first you are dazzled by the bright light, but only for a minute or so, while your pupils contract and the cells in your eyes turn their sensitivity down.

Your eyes also adjust to your surroundings by moving around, "scanning" different parts of the scene. As you look at this book, your eyes are moving many times a second, picking up details from a little bit of the page at a time. Your brain receives a stream of messages about these little bits, combines them, and you see the whole page all at once.

NIGHT VISION ▲

Owls and cats have eyes that are very sensitive to dim light, allowing them to hunt for food at night. Although night vision in humans is not as good, it is still remarkable. Your eyes have 200 million special cells called rods that help you see in the dark. The rods are so sensitive that they can detect the light of a single match lit 50 miles (80 km) away on a perfectly clear, pitch-dark night. They also let you see very well on a dark night deep in the country, with only the moon and stars for light. But rods do not adjust quickly to the dark; they take about 40 minutes to work effectively.

VIDEO MIXING ▶

Mixing a video involves watching several TV screens at once. Video editors have to spot when something important happens on a screen, even when they are not looking straight at it. They can do this by keeping their eyes moving all the time, helping them see things out of the corner of their eye. When their eyes stop moving, they can only take in the details of what is in front of them. Everything else is indistinct and may be missed.

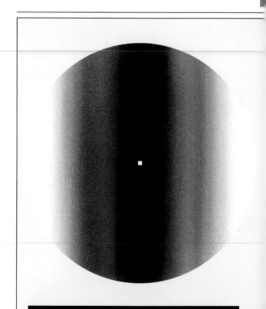

THE FADING BAR

In this picture (above), you can easily see a dark bar with fuzzy edges running down the middle of the circle. Now gaze steadily at the small white dot in the center of the circle. If you keep your eyes steady enough, the black bar will fade away after 10 seconds or so, and the whole circle will seem to be the same shade. If you move your eyes just a little, the bar will snap back into view again. You can see what a difference it makes to have movable eyes.

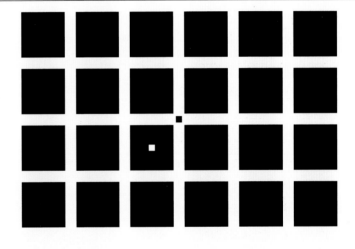

Brain Games

CAN YOU KEEP YOUR EYES STILL?

Stare at the black dot in the middle of the pattern (right) for 30 seconds, without changing your gaze. Now switch your gaze straight to the white dot nearby and stare at it. You will see an "afterimage"—a grid of bright lines crossing the dark squares—that will last for 5 to 10 seconds. The afterimage will jiggle around, no matter how hard you try to keep it centered on the white dot. This is because your eyes are always moving slightly, even when you think you are keeping them still.

EYE DOMINANCE

Look straight at a nearby object (above) and then hold up a finger about an inch (2.5 cm) in front of it so that object and finger are lined up. Now close each eye in turn. When you look with your "dominant" eye, they should still be lined up—with the other eye, they will go out of line.

READING IN THE DARK

All the letters in this picture (right) are easy to read in bright light. Go into a dark room (not completely dark—there should be some light coming in around the door and curtains). At first, you won't be able to read the letters, but after a few minutes the largest ones should be visible. Wait a little longer for your eyes to adjust. What is the smallest letter you can see now? What can you see after half an hour?

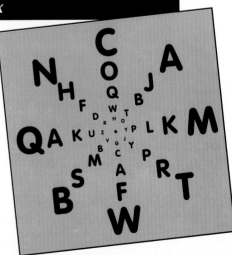

43

How Much Detail Can You See?

When you look at something, you see a complete picture. You also see small details at the same time.

IMAGINE THAT YOU'RE looking at the outside of your house. You can easily see big parts of it—the roof, the windows, the door—and you can also see small details, like single bricks or a doorknob. If you stand very close to the house, you can no longer see all of it. Now imagine walking further away. After a little while you won't be able to make out the small details. The amount of detail you can see is limited by how far away something is. It also depends on whether your vision is properly focused, and whether you look straight at something or out of the corner of your eye.

AERIAL PHOTOGRAPHY ▶

This spy plane can take clear pictures of cities from a height of more than 12 miles (20 km) up in the air. At this distance, roads and houses would no longer be visible to the human eye. The plane is equipped with cameras with special telephoto lenses that "zoom in" to photograph objects too far away to be seen.

PAINTING WITH DOTS ◀

The artist who painted this picture has created the shapes and colors of people and objects by using tiny dots of paint of different colors. This style of painting is called "pointillism." It works because people look at the picture from far enough away not to notice the fine detail of the dots, but they can see the bigger shapes that the dots make.

STARRY, STARRY NIGHT

Very tiny, faint details are easiest to see if you don't look straight at them! Try this out on a clear, starry night like this (left) by finding a very faint star—it will be easier to see by looking a little to one side of it.

THE SMALL PRINT

One way of printing pictures and photographs (right) is to make them from lots of tiny dots. You can make out the dots with a magnifying glass (a tool for seeing more detail). Try this with pictures from different books, magazines, and newspapers. (Try it on words, too!)

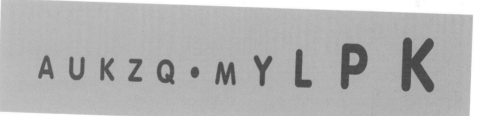

THE CORNER OF YOUR EYE

To see detail you need to look straight at something. If you look out of the corner of your eye, you can only make out large shapes. Keep your gaze steady on the spot in the middle of the chart (below), and do not move your eyes. On the right side, you will just be able to make out what all the letters are, but on the left side you will only be able to identify ones close to the spot. The further away something is from the point where your eyes are focused, the bigger it has to be in order for you to make out what it is. We don't usually have this problem because our eyes keep moving all the time.

A U K Z Q • M Y L P K

HORIZONTAL OR VERTICAL?

Try this simple test of your vision for detail. Look at these two patterns (left) from more than 20 feet (6 m) away. They will look the same. Now walk toward them. How close do you have to be before you can make out which is vertical and which is horizontal? Try it with one eye, then the other, and compare the results with those of your friends. If you wear glasses or contact lenses, try it without them on.

Is Seeing Always Believing?

Like it or not, sometimes we are fooled by what we see.

THINGS AREN'T ALWAYS what they seem. Your brain processes all the information sent by your eyes, but sometimes that information is misleading or confusing. What you think you see might not be what *really* enters your eyes. Have you ever felt dizzy at an amusement park—when you're not even on one of the rides? This can happen when you stare for a long time at a ride that's spinning around. When you look away everything else looks as though it is spinning and makes you feel dizzy. This is because your brain has been fooled by your eyes. Images that confuse our brains are called illusions. An illusion might fool one person, but not another. It all depends on how your brain makes sense of the information. Do the illusions on the opposite page fool you—or not?

THE WATERFALL ILLUSION ▶

If you gaze steadily at the center of a waterfall for a few minutes, and then look quickly away at an object, such as a tree, the object will seem to move upward for a few seconds. This happens because cells in the retina and brain that respond to downward motion get "tired." Only the cells that respond to upward motion still work, so the tree appears to move upward. This effect was first noticed at the Falls of Foyer in Scotland and is known as the "waterfall illusion."

Brain Games

WHICH IS BRIGHTER?

The inner circle appears to be lighter than the ring around it (right). But if you cover the edge of the inner circle with a circular strip of paper about a quarter of an inch (½ cm) wide, you will see that they are really the same shade. The darker shading around the edge of the inner circle causes the illusion.

SPOTS BEFORE YOUR EYES

As you look at the grid above, can you see pale gray patches where the white bars cross? They are most visible just to one side of where you are looking, which is why they seem to move as your gaze moves around. The patches are illusions produced by the cells in your retina and brain, which are fooled into combining the bright and dark areas of the picture.

HOW DARK IS IT?

The darkest parts of a TV picture are actually as light as the gray image that is left when you turn the TV off. This is because when the TV is on, pale parts of the picture make other parts seem dark by comparison (right). Try it and see for yourself.

THE WATERFALL ILLUSION ON TV

At the end of a TV show, stare at the center of the screen while the credits roll (below). When they stop, the picture will seem to move downward for a few seconds. Try using a VCR to find out what happens if you play the credits in reverse!

THE RETINAL COMPUTER ◀

The retina at the back of your eye is like a biological microchip. Light-sensitive cells in the retina connect to a network of nerve cells. This network carries out the first computations involved in extracting important information from the retinal image, and sends the results to the brain.

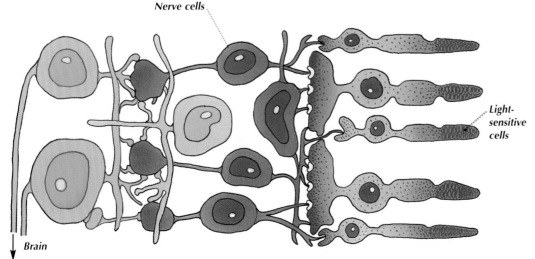

Nerve cells

Light-sensitive cells

Brain

Seeing in Your Head

Mental images are not just for daydreams; they can help us solve problems.

YOU KNOW THE experience of "seeing something that isn't there." It often happens in dreams and daydreams, which seem very real at the time. These pictures in your head are called mental images. They may seem to come from nowhere. But you can make your own mental images just by remembering or imagining something, and you can learn to move and change mental images deliberately as a way of solving puzzles. This skill—called visualization—seems to be a special talent, very different from intelligence. Some people have good visualization skills, while others, who are equally intelligent, do not.

ARTIST AT WORK ▶

Artists, like this caricaturist, need good powers of mental imagery. They have to be able to picture the finished work in their heads, because they may want it to look different from what they can actually see.

VIRTUAL REALITY ◀

This architect is using a virtual reality system in which miniature TV screens are built into the goggles. The imaginary scene on the screen changes as he turns his head or walks. You may know about virtual reality from playing computer games. When you move a "mouse," or press arrow keys on a keyboard, the picture on the screen changes as if you were moving through a real scene. Virtual reality is useful to engineers and architects as a way of bringing their mental images to life without building expensive models. They can design a car or a building and then use a virtual reality system to "move" around it and inside it, and see what it looks like from any direction.

Brain Games

SPOT THE MISTAKE

Look at the picture on the left. The artist has made nine mistakes in drawing the scene. Can you find them? (Check the Answers page when you think you have found all of them.) This puzzle tests your ability to see or visualize how shapes should look compared with how they have been drawn. If you found all of the mistakes quickly, you are probably good at drawing.

IMAGERY AND MEMORY

You can use mental imagery to remember a list. One way is to imagine funny pictures (below) of things you want to remember, such as weekend tasks (hand-washing a woolen sweater, doing homework, feeding the fish, and inviting a friend for dinner). This method can also help you remember shopping lists or facts for exams.

COMPLETE THE PICTURE

The picture below just seems to be a lot of black and white patches. But keep looking at it, and you should see something familiar. (If you can't, look at the Answers page.) When you've seen it once, or know what to look for, the object is easy to see, because you can form a mental image to help you find it.

COUNTING SIDES

How well can you use mental imagery? Look at each of the four shapes above, and count how many sides each shape has (not just the ones you can see, but also the ones out of sight). To do this, you have to "turn" the object around in your mind and imagine seeing it from other directions. Check your results on the Answers page.

49

Objects and Backgrounds

All by itself, your brain has learned complicated rules for telling objects and backgrounds apart.

AN IMAGE OF A SCENE in front of you falls on the retina at the back of your eye. The image is broken down by the millions of light-sensitive cells in your retina, each cell responding to the color and brightness of the light in a tiny patch of the image. But instead of seeing a confusing jumble of the patches of light, you see separate objects standing out against a background. Your brain knows that "objects" are things that are surrounded, and that "backgrounds" are the surrounding space. It also knows that the patterns covering the surface of an object have different shapes, colors, and sizes from those covering the background. This helps it separate the two. You can see how your brain does all this by trying these games in which it is sometimes difficult to tell objects and backgrounds apart.

Brain Games

FLOATING RECTANGLE

When you look at this drawing (below), you see what appears to be a rectangle floating on the page. But look carefully at the gaps between the circles. The edges of the rectangle that you expect to see aren't actually there. Your brain has automatically linked together the shaded parts of the circles to give the illusion of a rectangle.

GOING DOTTY

Are the red dots (right) grouped horizontally or vertically? How about the green dots and the blue dots (below)? The rows of red dots could be grouped either way, because they are evenly spaced. Wider spaces divide the green dots into four clear rows. The blue dots can easily be grouped by their colors.

SPIRAL ILLUSION ▶

When you look at this drawing, you immediately see a spiral pattern standing out against the background. But now try to trace the spiral with your finger. It isn't there! The short curved lines really make circles. Your brain, confused by the background, mistakenly links the short lines and interprets them as a foreground image—the nonexistent spiral.

SKULL OR DRINKERS? ◀

When you first look at this picture, you probably see a skull. But keep looking, especially around the "eyes" and "teeth"—can you see two people leaning toward each other over a table covered with glasses? Once you do, you'll find that you can flip back and forth between seeing one thing and the other—though you won't be able to see both at once! Your brain is jumping between deciding that the two big dark patches are part of the background of the skull, or part of the foreground of the scene with the two drinkers.

WHICH IS THE PROPELLER?

In these figures (right), do you see a green propeller against a white background, or do you see a white propeller against a green background? Which of these pictures makes it easiest to see a white propeller? Try making your own drawings to find out what happens with different propeller sizes.

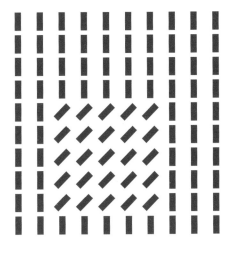

FIND THE SQUARE

The two grids (left) both contain a square made from pieces that contrast with the rest. The square in the far-left grid "jumps out" at you, but can you find the one in the near-left grid? Small differences between the pieces of a picture sometimes stand out immediately. But this doesn't always happen, and we may have to search for the differences. (See the Answers page.)

Nature's Illusions

To survive, many animals have evolved to look like their backgrounds, or like something else entirely! Some disguises can fool human experts as well as the animal's enemies or prey.

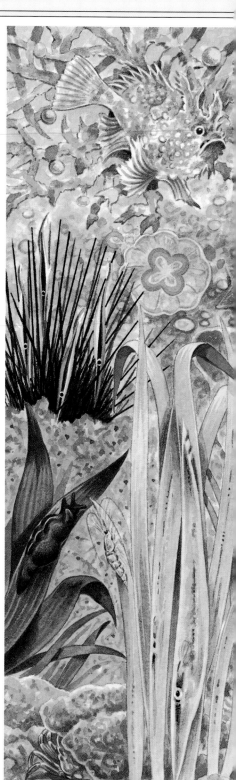

FOR MOST ANIMALS, keeping out of the way of predators is a matter of life and death. If its predators hunt by vision, then an animal will have a better chance of surviving if it is hard to see against its background. For predators, it is easier to capture prey if the prey can't see them coming. This is the simple reason for animal camouflage, but there are as many kinds of camouflage as there are animals. Some camouflaged animals have the same color and texture as their background. This allows them to blend into the scenery even if they are as big as polar bears. Others have markings that seem to attract attention but actually make them harder to see. Others resemble things that are inedible or poisonous.

STANDING OUT TO BLEND IN ▼

Some animals are covered in markings that make the outline of their whole body harder to see. This is called disruptive coloration. The black and white stripes of a zebra look conspicuous to us, but in fact they provide a very effective form of camouflage. When a group of zebras are together, the confusing patterns of the stripes make it difficult for a lion or other predator to pick out a single target for attack.

MILITARY CAMOUFLAGE ◀

Nature's trick of using disruptive color markings has been copied by military equipment designers. The plane in the picture is camouflaged with the same patchwork of colors as the ground beneath it. This makes it difficult to see from above, where an enemy pilot may be cruising. The underside of a camouflaged plane is painted a smooth pale gray or blue, making it harder to see from below against the background of the sky. This protects it from spotters on the ground. Both ideas are borrowed from nature—fish often have different camouflage on their backs and their bellies.

Brain Games

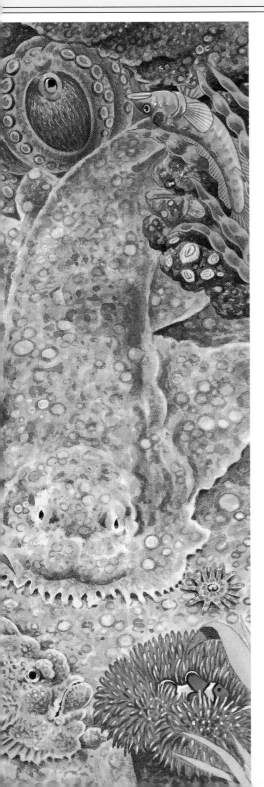

FIND THE ANIMALS

In the imaginary underwater scene on the left, there are 18 camouflaged marine animals. See how many you can find among the rocks, sand, and seaweed. Turn to the Answers page to check if you are right. Would you make a good underwater predator? (If you were a predator, you would probably be camouflaged yourself!)

FALSE IDENTITY

Look at the pictures below and try to decide what an animal would think each one is. With this form of camouflage, animals protect themselves by appearing to be something they are not—something that does not interest their predators. Turn to the Answers page to find out what they are.

Color

To see colors, our eyes and brains must respond differently to different kinds of light rays.

THE LIGHT THAT comes from the sun or an electric light is made up of light rays with different wavelengths. Under white or natural light, objects of different colors absorb some of these wavelengths and reflect only the wavelength of the color you see. In other words, a banana absorbs all the wavelengths except yellow, so it appears yellow to your eyes. Most people's eyes have three kinds of light receptors (cones), and each works best in light of a different wavelength: short, medium, or long, for blue, green, and red. These are the primary (main) colors of light. White light—"pure" light—is made up of all the wavelengths or colors together.

PRISMS

A prism is a specially cut piece of glass that "splits" white light into all the colors of the spectrum. It does this by bending some wavelengths more than others. The long wavelengths are bent the least; when they fall on a white screen, it looks red. The short wavelengths are bent the most, and they look violet. The whole sequence of colors in the spectrum is red, orange, yellow, green, blue, indigo, and violet. Light with wavelengths outside this range is invisible to human eyes (but not to some animals). If its wavelength is longer than red light, it is called infrared; if the wavelength is shorter than violet light, it is called ultraviolet.

WHY SEE IN COLOR?

Seeing in color helps animals survive in their natural environments. Many animals feed on fruits, nuts, and berries, and it can be difficult to spot these quickly in a large mass of leaves. Color vision makes it easier, because the animal can see the difference between the leaves and the fruit. The greater the contrast, the easier it is to see the fruit. Can you think of some things that would be more difficult for you to do if you couldn't

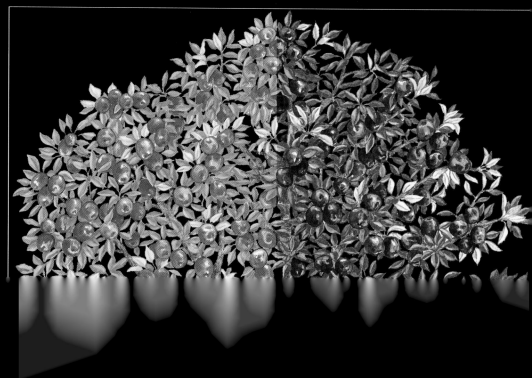

Brain Games

COLORBLINDNESS

Can you see a number in the pattern of dots on the left? Don't worry if you cannot—lots of people are red-green colorblind, which only means that they can't tell some colors apart because their eyes have only two kinds of cones instead of three. About four percent of all people are colorblind—mostly males. (The answer is on the Answers page.)

NEGATIVE AFTERIMAGES

Stare at the center of the cross in the blue circle (above) for 20 seconds, then look at the dot in the gray square. Let your eyes recover, then repeat the steps with the yellow circle and the gray square. What did you see? These brief "afterimages" appear in the complementary color to the color you stared at. (Complementary colors produce white light when mixed.) Yellow and blue are complementary, and so are green and magenta (a dark purple-red). You see afterimages because the cells carrying messages from your eyes to your brain take time to adjust to a new color after seeing the same color for a while.

COLOR AFTERIMAGES

Look at the black and white pattern below—there are no colors in it. Now stare at the red lines on the right for 10 seconds, then at the green lines in the middle for 10 seconds. Keep repeating this for at least three minutes (5–10 minutes if you have enough patience). When you're finished, look at the black and white pattern again. What color are the lines now? Your brain has linked the direction of the lines with their color. Look at the black and white pattern again an hour later, and the pale "afterimage" colors will probably still be there!

COLORS AND BACKGROUNDS

In the squares on the right are four colors against two different backgrounds, black and white. Look carefully at each pair of colored squares, one at a time. Are they the same color, or does one row look brighter? The colors you see aren't just a matter of the wavelengths of light bouncing off objects. Your brain is also influenced by the colors in the surrounding area. In this case, the colors look much more vivid with a black background than with a white one.

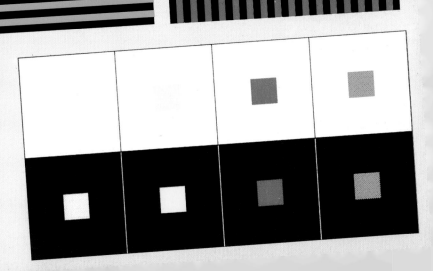

Seeing in Color

What colors you can see depends on light-sensitive cells in your eyes. The same is true for animals.

MANY ANIMALS SEE COLORS, but they may see them in different ways. Birds, bees, cats, and humans, for example, all have different color vision because they have different kinds of eyes. Their eyes all have special cells called cones that "see" color—they are sensitive to different wavelengths of light. Cats' and dogs' eyes have only two kinds of cones. This means that they can't distinguish some colors that humans can. Birds have four or more different kinds of cone, so two different berries might look the same color to you, but they would look very different to a blackbird. Many animals have cones sensitive to ultraviolet light, which is invisible to humans. For bees, the three primary colors detected by their cones are green, blue, and ultraviolet.

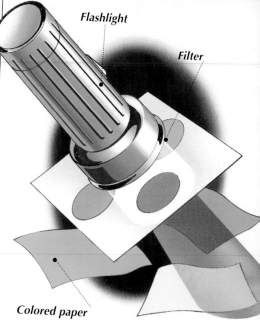

Flashlight

Filter

Colored paper

INDOORS AND OUTDOORS ▲

Ordinary cameras cannot adjust for changes in the color of light, and you have to use different film for taking pictures in daylight and in artificial light. Both these pictures were taken with the same daylight film—the outdoor scene looks normal, but the indoor one has far too much red and orange in it. This is because the light from an electric light bulb has more red wavelengths, and fewer blue wavelengths, than sunlight. Your brain adjusts to this difference automatically—if it didn't, a piece of white paper would look slightly blue in daylight and orange under electric light! Your brain can't compensate perfectly, though, which explains why it is sometimes difficult to choose the color of clothes or paint under artificial light.

COLOR CONSTANCY

You will need a flashlight (above), a piece of white cardboard, and some flat pieces of colored plastic. You also need some squares of plain colored paper and a colorful picture. Make a filter for the flashlight by cutting circles in the white cardboard and putting a piece of plastic at the back of each circle. In a very dark room, look at the squares one by one under the colored light, beginning with a pale filter (such as yellow). What happens to the squares? Now look at the picture under the same filter. Does the same thing happen? When you see many colors at once, your brain compensates for the flashlight, and the colors look the same as in normal light.

BEE VISION

Bees feed on nectar from flowers, and they need to be able to tell from a distance which flowers are worth visiting. They do this by spotting the pattern of colors on the petals. Because the light-sensitive cells in a bee's eye are different from ours, color patterns on petals may look very different to you and to a bee. Some flowers have petals that look pure white to humans; but there are patches on these petals that reflect different amounts of ultraviolet light. So to a bee, they have very obvious dark markings, making them easy to tell apart.

Brain Games

FLOWER SHOW

During the spring or summer, try this simple experiment on bees' color vision. Cut out flower shapes (below) from thin colored cardboard. (Make sure you use at least red, yellow, green, and blue.) Put a plastic bottlecap full of sugared water in the centers. Find a clump of real flowers that is being visited by lots of bees, and arrange the cardboard flowers nearby. Watch patiently. Bees will land on the cardboard flowers to investigate. Count how many visits each one gets. Which is the bees' favorite color?

COLORED DOTS

At normal reading distance, the red, blue, and black dots on the left are easy to tell apart. Now prop up the book at slightly more than arm's length away and look again. The red dots stand out clearly, but it is harder to tell which are black and which are blue. This is because the light receptors in your eyes that are sensitive to blue are thinly scattered over the back of your retina, so it is harder to tell blue from black in the small details of a pattern seen from a distance.

MAKE YOUR OWN RAINBOW

When sun shines through raindrops, the raindrops break up the light in the same way that a prism does, making a rainbow. You can make your own rainbow (right) by putting a glass of water on a window sill in bright sunlight, with the glass slightly over the edge of the sill. Put a large sheet of white paper on the floor below the window, and you will see a rainbow pattern of colors falling on it.

Seeing in Depth

When your brain combines the messages from your two eyes, it helps you see a solid world—one with depth.

WHEN SCIENTISTS FIRST DISCOVERED how our eyes work, they were puzzled by many things. Why did the world look solid, even though the images formed on the retina at the back of the eye were flat? How did people make out shapes, and tell how far away they were? We now know that it helps to have two eyes, which give us binocular vision. The right eye and the left eye have a slightly different view of the world, forming different images on the retina. The closer you are to something, the more different it looks to each of your eyes. Our ability to know where things are in relation to us is called depth perception, and it helps us see a solid world. Some of the Brain Games opposite show how flat pictures can be made to look solid if you look at different parts of the pictures with each eye. In infancy, our brains become "wired up" to combine the messages from the two eyes. About five percent of people will not be able to see the effects here.

THE CIRCLING PENDULUM

Make a pendulum (above) with a lump of clay or rubber hanging from a piece of thread, and set it swinging back and forth across your line of vision. If you put one lens of a pair of dark glasses in front of one of your eyes, the pendulum will seem to circle, swinging alternately nearer and farther from you as it goes back and forth. Take the dark glasses away, and you will see that it is really still swinging straight! The pendulum appears to move in a circle because the dark glass slows down the messages to one of your eyes.

SEEING DOUBLE

Look steadily at an object about an arm's length away. Now hold a pencil upright and move it back and forth between the object and your nose, always keeping your gaze on the object. At a certain point you will notice that the pencil magically becomes two pencils.

FLAT OR SOLID? ▶

When you look at the moon, you see a flat disk, although it is really a solid sphere. This is because the moon is too far away for there to be any noticeable difference between its images in each of your eyes; and without slightly different images in each eye, you cannot see that it has depth. Your eyes would have to be several thousand miles apart to see the moon as solid! A powerful lens was used for this picture.

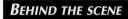

Brain Games

(See the Answers page if you are not sure.)

BEHIND THE SCENE

Hold this picture (left) so that it touches your nose. Let your eyes relax, and stare "through the picture" into space. Now move the page slowly to arm's length, still staring through it all the time. After a few tries, you should see a hidden object in the design. Can you tell what it is? (See the Answers page if you are not sure.)

COMBINING TWO IMAGES

Stare at a point between the two drawings (right), trying to look "through the page" into the distance. At first, you'll just see double images, but if you are patient you may be able to make the two images come together in the middle, and see a solid object coming out of the page toward you.

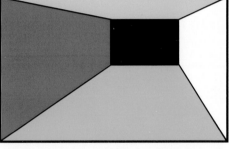 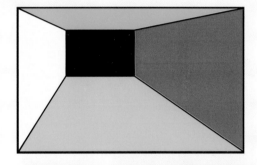

Left eye view

Right eye view

JUMPING OBJECTS

Look at a nearby object, such as a computer (left). Open one eye and close the other, over and over. The object seems to jump from side to side. Things closer to you jump more than things further away, because up close there is more difference between the view in each eye.

3-D THRILLS ▶

In some sci-fi and horror films of the 1950s, monsters seemed to burst out of the screen at the audience. This trick was set up by taking two films from slightly different angles, printing one in red and one in green, and having audiences look at them with a red filter over one eye and a green filter over the other. Each eye sees just one of the pictures, and the scene appears solid.

Depth and Perspective

The rules of perspective used in drawing help us understand the layout of things around us.

YOUR BRAIN COMBINES the information from your two eyes about the relative size and positions of parts of what you are looking at to enable you to judge distances. For instance, when you walk down a street, your eyes pass information to your brain about the cars, people, and buildings so you don't bump into things.

Until about 500 years ago, artists did not know how to show distance in their paintings. Pictures tended to look flat and lacking in depth. Then the rules of perspective were discovered—rules of drawing that enabled artists to give their pictures depth. Now they could draw a road winding into the distance or a person's arm reaching toward you. These rules are still used today. Try the Brain Games to find out more about perspective.

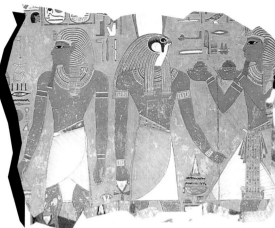

A FLAT WORLD ▲

Artists in ancient Egypt painted this scene thousands of years ago, before the rules of perspective were discovered. The figures look flat, and the scene has no depth.

IMPOSSIBLE PICTURE

Here is an amazing picture (left) in which the normal rules of perspective are not being used correctly, making it an "impossible" scene. How many things can you find wrong with the picture? There are at least 10 to look for. When you think you have found them all, turn to the Answers page to see if you are right.

VANISHING POINT ▶

Although we know that parallel lines never meet, when we see them in the real world they *appear* to converge at a point known as the vanishing point. The lines on the drawing of this photograph show where it is. Since the discovery of this rule of perspective, artists have used the vanishing point to give pictures depth.

Vanishing point

Brain Games

WHICH IS WIDER?

Which of the two crossbars (below) is longer? Measure them, and you'll find they are the same length. They appear to be different lengths because the brain is tricked by the visual clues about perspective. We expect the upper bar to be longer because it stretches across four lines instead of two.

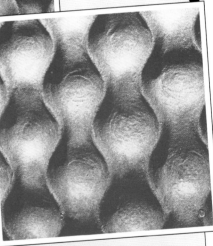

WHICH WAY UP?

Look at the two photographs of egg boxes (above). The lower one appears to be the right way up, as if you could put eggs in it. Now turn the page upside down. What happens? In fact, both photographs are of egg boxes the right way up, but the lower one has been lit from above. We unconsciously use shadows to judge the shapes and depths of objects, and assume that the light is coming from above.

Seeing Things Move

Your eyes depend on your brain to interpret moving objects. This is more difficult if you are moving too.

WHEN THINGS around you move, their images on the backs of your eyes move too. Your brain is able to figure out from these changing images what is moving, how fast it is moving, and in what direction. It can do this quickly enough for you to roller-skate, dodge a snowball, or play a computer game. Sometimes your brain can be tricked, so that you see movement when there really is none, or you see the wrong thing move. There are even times when your brain tells you that you are moving, even though you are still. This happens when everything around you moves, but your brain assumes that the movement of the image on the eye has happened because you are moving.

ANIMATION ▼

As you watch a film, you see the picture move. You are actually being shown one slightly different still picture after another. Because they change 24 times a second, you don't see each one disappear and then another one appear. Instead, you see a continuously moving scene. Special high-speed film is needed to show movement in still pictures like these.

WHICH IS MOVING? ▼

When you look at a small object against a bigger background, your brain assumes that the background is always still. If there is any movement, it seems to be the object and not the background that is moving. Usually this is right, but not always! On a windy night when clouds are blowing across the sky, look at the moon as the clouds pass in front of it. It will look as if the moon is racing past the clouds.

Brain Games

THE MOVING DOT

Cover the end of a flashlight (right) with dark tape. Prop it on a table to keep it still, and make a tiny hole in the tape with a pin. Stare at the dot of light from across a completely dark room, keeping your head still. What happens to the dot? Your brain is tricked into seeing it move because your eyes continue to move slightly in the dark.

PUT THE FISH IN THE BOWL

Draw a fish on one piece of cardboard and a bowl of water on another (left). Fasten the edges of the cards together, with the pictures facing out. Leave enough room to attach a thin stick or a pencil firmly in the center. Spin the stick rapidly. Because your brain sees both sides at once, the fish jumps into the bowl!

MAKE YOUR OWN CARTOON

To see how animation works, try making a simple cartoon (above). You will need a pad of paper that you can flick through quickly with your thumb (either a notepad or some unlined index cards stapled together at the far edge will do). On each sheet, draw a simple object such as a small circle a little higher each time, then a little lower, and so on. Now flick the pad. What do you see?

OLD-FASHIONED HOME MOVIES

Start with a strip of cardboard about 38 inches (96 cm) long and 5 inches (12 cm) high. Draw a series of pictures like the ones shown below along the strip, and cut slits in the sides (be careful not to cut the pictures!). Fold the strip into a circle and make a matching cardboard circle to put underneath it. Attach the strip to the circle and paint the outside black. Put a pin through the center of the circle and attach it to a cork. Put the cork in a bottle for stability, and stand it under a light. To see the action, spin the disk and look through the slits.

Light from lamp

Pin with cork attached underneath the cardboard

Optical Illusions

Optical illusions trick your brain into making wrong conclusions. Here are some ways to create them.

MOST OF THE TIME, you don't make mistakes about what you are seeing. You can tell what things are, whether they are moving or still, and how big or how far away they are. This is because real, three-dimensional scenes give your eyes and brain plenty of information. If there is any doubt, you can move closer or look again. It is much more difficult when you are looking at a picture. Over the years, people have discovered lots of ways to make pictures in which things appear to be different in size or shape from what they really are. In these pictures, you often cannot tell how big something is, or how far away it is, and your brain is tricked into "seeing" what is not there.

CAT-SIZED SHRIMP? ▲

Shrimp come in different sizes—but is this a picture of a cat and a very large shrimp, or a normal shrimp and a miniature cat? In real life this scene would be impossible to fake without models, but the picture is possible if the cat is photographed from a distance and the shrimp is photographed from close-up, with nothing else to compare them to. (The shrimp is less than 2½ inches, or 6 cm, long.)

KING KONG ◀

King Kong was made using trick photography. For the scenes of Kong towering over buildings, two different films were spliced together: one of the city, and one of the gorilla. When this film was made, the techniques were not as good as they are now. The woman in Kong's hand is much too big for this scene to be realistic. In another scene, Kong is shown climbing up one of these buildings.

Brain Games

SPINNING DISK

Draw two circles, each about 3½ inches (9 cm) across (left) close together on a piece of cardboard, then draw two pictures in the circles like the ones shown here. (One of them must be upside down.) Cut the circles out, leaving them joined in the center, and glue them back to back to make a disk. Make two holes at opposite edges of the disk. Cut two pieces of string 16 inches (40 cm) long. Thread one string through each hole and tie its ends together. Twist the strings rapidly between your fingers to spin the disk. The drawings on each side of the disk seem to combine into a complete picture!

MOVING W

Fold a rectangular sheet of paper (right) into four equal sections and stand it on a table in a W shape. Keeping your head still, look at it with one eye shut and try to make it "reverse," so that the two corners marked with dots in the picture seem to be at the top of the shape, not on the table. (This may take a while!) Once you can keep the shape reversed, move your head slowly—you will see the piece of paper twist and turn as you move. This happens because your brain interprets the moving image on your eye incorrectly.

REVERSING ARROW

Draw an arrow facing right on a piece of paper (below) and prop it upright on a table. Place a glass of water in front of it, stand back a little, and look at the arrow through the glass. Which way is it facing now? This optical illusion happens because rays of light are bent before they reach your eye. Other illusions happen for the same kind of reason. For example, when a road looks shiny on a hot day, what you are really seeing is the sky reflected by a layer of hot air!

OPTICAL ZOO-LUSION

This is a double drawing (below). As it is shown here, the top section looks like a very strange muddle. But if you put the bars over the muddled drawing and slide them from side to side, you will see two completely different animals in turn. To make this "moving zoo" optical illusion work, carefully trace the bars onto a piece of thick paper, making them exactly the same size as they are here. Then cut out the spaces between the bars. Last of all, fit the bars over the picture and slide them back and forth. What two animals do you see in the cage?

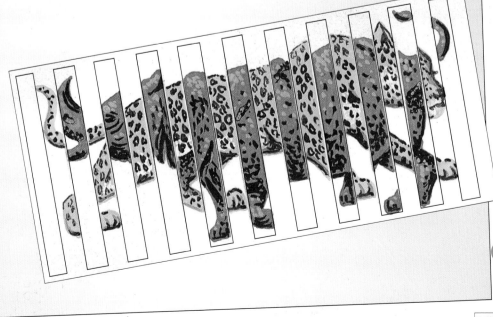

Geometric Illusions

Optical illusions can also play tricks when you look at simple shapes.

SOME ILLUSIONS work by not giving you complete information about a scene. Others work by giving two or more sets of information that seem to match up until you look closely! This is often more obvious in geometric shapes. When you try to judge the length of a line in a drawing, or the size of an angle, your brain is influenced by other parts of the drawing, and it is impossible to make yourself see only the part you need to see. Designers learn this. When in doubt, they check length with a ruler.

WHICH WAY IS UP? ▶

A journey through this "House of Stairs" is difficult to make, because the stairs don't take you anywhere. The artist plays tricks with perspective and creates a scene that looks realistic until you try to connect the different parts by following the stairs.

IMPOSSIBLE SHAPES ▼

The two drawings below are simpler examples of "impossible" shapes. They seem to be three-dimensional shapes. When you look at them more closely, you can see that the lines do not connect as they should. Actually, the shapes are flat (two-dimensional), but your brain tries to make them three-dimensional as if they were real objects.

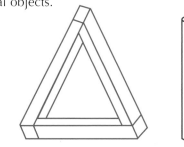

Brain Games

WHICH IS TALLER?

Is the corner of the room taller than the corner of the building (below)? Measure them both with a ruler. (Measure all the way to the carpet.) The room seems taller because the angles at the top and bottom seem to open out, drawing your eye with them.

MAKE A SLIDE RULE

Fold a piece of cardboard in half lengthwise and tape the long edge closed to form a tube (right). On one side, draw a two-headed arrow measuring 2½ inches (6 cm) between the points, with one point touching one end of the tube. On the back, draw a scale exactly 2½ inches (6 cm), with one end touching the same end as the arrow on the other side. Take another piece of cardboard of the same width and draw another arrow 2½ inches (6 cm) long, but with only one arrow—this one pointing in. On the back, mark off 2½ inches (6 cm) as if on a ruler. Put the second piece into the tube and ask a friend to slide it back and forth to try to make the two arrow figures the same length. Turn the tube over to check their judgment.

CIRCLE CONFUSION

Look at the circle pattern on the right. Are the two horizontal lines parallel, or do they bend away from the center of the circle? Check them with a ruler. You'll find that they don't actually bend, but are really straight and parallel to one another! Here, your impression of the shape of the lines is influenced by the pattern in the background, even after you know from using a ruler that the lines are really straight. Try drawing your own patterns. What kinds of background make the straight lines appear to bend?

A PERFECT SQUARE?

Is the shape in the middle of the picture (below) a square, with all four sides equal and right angles at its corners? Once you have decided, check your answer by measuring the lengths of the sides with a ruler. Now compare the angles with the corners of a rectangular sheet of paper. This illusion happens because the background pattern of lines makes you see the square in a different way. Your brain guesses that the square is standing upright on a flat surface, and uses the rules of perspective to interpret its shape.

BENT OR STRAIGHT?

Look at the figure below. Is the diagonal line straight, or is it slightly bent? When you are sure of the answer, check with a ruler. The rectangle that "interrupts" the line is what causes this illusion.

Memory Games

Images are thought to be much easier to remember than words or numbers. How good is your visual memory?

Y OUR BRAIN keeps memories of what the world around you looks like. Usually, you don't realize that you're doing this, because a stream of new information is coming in from your eyes all the time. But if the lights go out, or you close your eyes, you have to rely on your memory to know where things are around you, to pick something up or to stop yourself from tripping. All these memories are stored as pictures in your brain. There are many kinds of games you can play to find out more about your memory. The easiest things to remember are the ones you are most interested in.

PHOTOGRAPHIC MEMORY

S ome people have a "photographic memory"—they can remember lots of details about things that they have seen only once. To test your memory for details, look at the picture above for a few minutes. Then turn to the Answers page and try to answer the questions about this picture without looking back at this page. How well do you do?

DONKEY WORK ▲

W hen you play "Pin the Tail on the Donkey," you have to remember exactly where the donkey is so that when your eyes are covered, you can walk in the right direction and reach out to pin the tail in the right place. The player is usually spun around a few times after being blindfolded, because this makes it harder to remember which direction to go in. What else do you think might make the donkey harder to find? Test your ideas the next time you play the game.

NUMBERS AND MEMORY

L ook at one series of numbers below. Wait a minute, then without looking at it, try to write it down. Now try the other numbers, but first break the series down into short sections. You should find it much easier! Now try memorizing a new number that a friend has made up and read aloud. Do your eyes remember better than your ears?

14921793
01738526

Brain Games

TEST ON A TRAY

Play the game below to test your own and your friends' memories. Put a collection of common objects on a tray and show it to a friend for five seconds. Then ask them to shut their eyes and name as many of the objects as they can. Count how many they get right, and then switch over and try it yourself with a new set of objects. Who gets the highest score? What happens if you are distracted while you are trying to remember? After you close your eyes, try multiplying two-digit numbers in your head before saying what was on the tray. How much does your score go down?

WHAT DID YOU SEE?

How good are you at remembering exactly what something looks like? Look at the two drawings below for a few seconds. Wait a few minutes, then turn to the Answers page, where you will see six drawings. Only two of them are identical to the ones below. Can you tell which ones they are without looking back at this page?

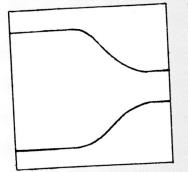

CARD SHARP

Spread out a deck of playing cards (above) face down. Take turns turning two cards over at a time, letting the other players see them. If the cards have the same value (for example, two nines or two jacks), you keep them and score a point. If they don't, put them back, face down. The game lasts until all the cards are matched in pairs. The winner has the most pairs.

Eye on the Ball

In some sports, you have to learn to use your eyes to hit, catch, kick, or jump accurately.

WHEN YOU REACH for a door handle, catch a falling glass, or jump over a puddle, your brain uses messages from your eyes to figure out how far away things are from you and how fast they or you are moving. Then it sends the right commands to your muscles, so that you reach the right way, or jump the right distance. When you play ball games or other sports, you need to reach, catch, and jump even more quickly and accurately.

By finding out how our brains use information from our eyes, scientists have discovered better ways of training athletes.

WHERE WILL IT FALL? ◄

When you are a fielder in a ball game like baseball, how do you know where to run to catch the ball? If the ball is hit low, it's easy, but a ball hit high up into the sky is more difficult. Professional fielders learn to run into a position that would be directly under the ball if it were climbing straight up. When the ball drops, they are right underneath it. Next time you watch a ball game, watch the fielders running to catch balls. Do they look where they are going, or do they look at the ball?

RETURNING A SERVE ▼

When you play tennis or baseball, you have to swing the racket or bat at exactly the right moment to hit a speeding ball. You also have to hit the ball in the right direction and for the right distance. To get it right, you must learn to control where you look. First keep your eye on the ball, then at just the right moment look at where you want the ball to go. The direction that your head and eyes are pointing is very important!

Brain Games

HOW MANY COINS?

Bend your arm in the same way as in the picture (left) and balance a stack of coins on your elbow. How high can you make the stack before the coins fall off? While you're trying to balance them, keep your eyes on the stack so that you can see if it is wobbling. Once you've got a tall stack just balanced, turn your head and look away. What happens? Is it just as easy to keep the coins balanced now?

DON'T SPILL IT!

Fill a glass up to the brim with water and walk around holding it (right). Keep it steady and don't spill any water. Now, try to do the same thing without looking at the glass. Can you still walk without spilling any water, or do you need to look at the glass to keep it steady? (Be sure to try this outdoors.)

ONE-HANDED JUGGLING

Throw a ball up into the air a few times, and catch it in one hand (above). Now, try shutting your eyes while the ball is falling toward your hand. You'll find that you can catch the ball perfectly well with your eyes shut, provided you close them only just before you catch. If you close your eyes any sooner, you'll usually miss the ball. By switching the lights out while people catch balls, scientists have found that you have to be able to see the ball until three-tenths of a second before you catch it. After that, it doesn't matter whether you can see it or not!

FLIP AND CATCH

Put a small place mat on the edge of a table, partly sticking out over the edge. Flick it into the air by bringing your hand up quickly underneath it (below), then try to catch it with the same hand before it lands again. Once you can do it every time, try it while looking away, or use several mats.

LONG JUMPING

How do long jumpers hit the takeoff board with one foot so accurately every time (below)? Find out by setting up your own long jump. (You don't have to jump to do this experiment.) You need a surface such as damp sand where you can see your footprints. Make a mark on the ground and run or walk toward it several times, each time bringing your foot right onto the mark. Measure the distances between your last 5–10 strides. How many strides back do you start to shorten or lengthen your pace? Most trained athletes start to adjust their pace three strides back—keeping their eyes on the takeoff board as they run.

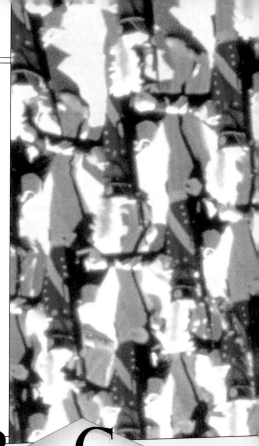

That Looks Familiar

Familiar sights—whether they're faces or objects—are easy to take for granted. What helps you identify them?

MOST OF THE TIME, you have no trouble telling what things are when you see them. But it can be more difficult when you see something from an unusual angle, or in a situation where you don't expect to see it. Your brain relies on things being in their usual places and positions to help you identify them quickly, without having to puzzle over them. Something we're all especially good at is recognizing other people's faces. When you think about how little difference there is between one face and another, it is amazing that you can recognize hundreds or even thousands of different faces.

Brain Games

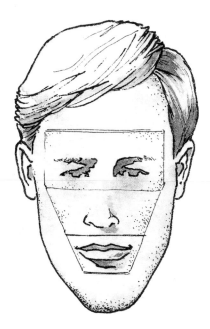

WANTED: THIS FACE ▲

Identikit (Photofit) is used to help witnesses to crimes make a picture of the face of the person wanted by the police. The kit consists of lots of photographs of different mouths, noses, eyes, chins, and hairlines, which fit together to make many different faces. The witness tries combinations of these photographs to find the one that looks most like the face they remember.

GUESS WHO?

Whose face is in this drawing (left)? Take a good look before you turn the book upside down to check. (If you are still puzzled, look on the Answers page.) Most things are equally easy to recognize either way up, but upside down faces usually take a little longer to identify. This may be because from the time we are born we mostly see other people's faces the right way up.

GUESS WHO AGAIN!

Who is this (right)? You probably can't tell. But if you hold the picture away from you and squint to blur your vision, you may be able to recognize the face. If you wear glasses or contact lenses, try it without them. The photograph has been processed by a computer to divide it into small squares and make the colors run together. If you still can't tell who it is, turn to the Answer page to find out.

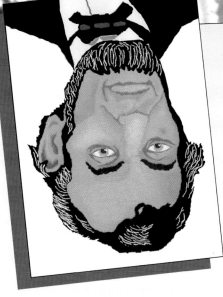

MARCHING UPSIDE DOWN ◀

This picture looks like just a lot of triangles, squares and other colored shapes, but it is a photograph of a real-life scene. There are several things that make it difficult to tell what it is. First, the photograph is blurred. Second, it is upside down. (If you turn the page upside down you will see what it is immediately.) Also, all the people are marching close together, seeming to form one large pattern, so it is very difficult to pick out individual people and uniforms. Finally, there is no background to provide more clues.

A STRANGE FACE

What is peculiar about this face (left)? At first it looks like an upside-down picture of a normal face, but look carefully. (If you are not sure, check the Answers page.) You can make your own strange faces with pictures cut out of magazines.

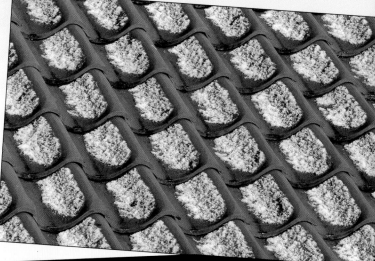

WHAT PLANET IS THIS?

Photographs taken from hundreds of miles out in space by satellites can be used to make maps of the surfaces of planets. This map (below) has been made from satellite photographs, but there is something slightly unusual about it that makes it different from most maps. Which planet do you think it shows? (Hint: if you figure out what is unusual about it, that should tell you immediately which planet it is.) When you think you know, turn to the Answers page to check.

WHAT IS IT?

What are you looking at (above)? It is difficult to know because of the way the photograph has been taken. If you saw this scene in real life, you would know right away what it was, because you would see all of its surroundings at the same time. Once you've taken your best guess, turn to the Answers page to check.

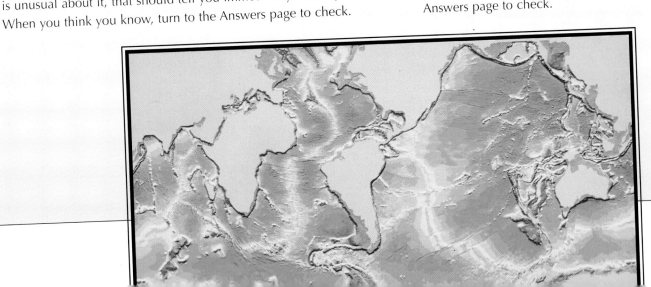

Answers

FILLING KNOWLEDGE GAPS   PAGE 4

Square = 3, circle = 2, triangle = 4, star = 5. The missing number is 14. To find the missing number without cracking the code, subtract the sum of the numbers down the side (35) from the sum of the numbers along the bottom (49).

WHICH SWITCH?   PAGE 4

Switch on the first switch and leave it on for two minutes before turning it off. Then switch on the next switch and leave it on for just 15 seconds before turning it off. Now feel the three light bulbs. The hottest bulb will be connected to the first switch you tried, the cooler one to the second, and the cold one to the unused switch.

FIND THE QUICKEST ROUTE   PAGE 5

To figure out the time it takes to get from one point to the next, divide the distance by the speed. The quickest route is this one: Home to f (5 m ÷ 2 mph = 2.5 hours); f to g (5 m ÷ 3 mph = 1.67 hours); g to red flag (15 m ÷ 2 mph = 7.5 hours); red flag to blue flag (8 m ÷ 5 mph = 1.6 hours). But it would be quicker to send out two separate parties to the two sites.

WHAT IS THE LONGEST SPAN?   PAGE 7

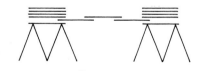

Hint: put small weights such as coins on the cards to strengthen the bridge.

DESIGN A SPINNER   PAGE 7

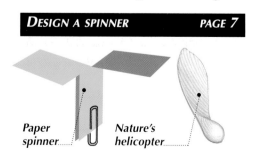

Paper spinner   Nature's helicopter

A CODING DEVICE   PAGE 7

On the inner ring of the disk, read the letter one (or more) spaces to the right of the letter on the outer ring.

SALTY, SWEET, SOUR, OR BITTER?   P. 9

The map of your tongue should look something like this one. SA = salty; SO = sour; SW = sweet; BI = bitter.

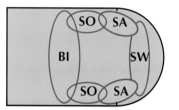

WHAT IS THE MISSING CARD?   PAGE 9

You only need to look through the deck three times to figure out which card is missing. The first time, count all the black cards. If there are 25 you know the missing card is black; if there are 26 you know it is red. If the missing card is black, count all the spades. If there are 13 you know the missing card is a club; if there are 12 you know it is a spade. Finally, when you know the suit, go through the suit to see which one is missing. Count aces as one, jacks as 11, queens as 12, and kings as 13. Subtract the numbers from 91 to leave the number of the missing card.

RECOGNITION   PAGE 9

The three objects are, clockwise from the top: a cheese grater, a pepper mill, and an electric hair dryer.

CRYPTARITHMETIC   PAGE 11

If X = 5, then W = 0, T = 1, S = 8, and J = 2.

MATCHING FACES   PAGE 11

The three pairs are: 1 and 5; 3 and 4; 2 and 6.

READING BAD HANDWRITING   PAGE 11

The chemical formulas written in bad handwriting are: $Fe_4[Fe(CN)_6]_3$, $Na_2SiO_4.xH_2O$, and $CaSO_4.\frac{1}{2}H_2O$.

CRACK THE PRICE CODE   PAGE 11

L = 0, M = 1, N = 2, K = 3, P = 4, Q = 6, R = 7, S = 8, T = 9.

WHICH BARBER?   PAGE 12

John should go to the barber with the bad haircut. If each barber cuts the other one's hair, the one with the bad haircut must be the good barber!

RED AND BLUE STICKERS   PAGE 13

If one person had been given a red sticker, the other one would see it and know that their own sticker was blue. If neither person reacts immediately, they must both have blue stickers.

MAKING CONNECTIONS   PAGE 14

You can press any two switches to make the star-shaped light go on.

NUMBERS GAME   PAGE 14

E.

ATTENTION TO DETAIL   PAGE 15

Star = 20, square = 30, oval = 49, rectangle = 30. There are 68 balls altogether.

SPOT THE DIFFERENCE   PAGE 15

WHAT COMES NEXT?   PAGE 15

The next shape in the sequence is 3. The shape that completes the box is D.

HIDDEN TRIANGLES   PAGE 17

We found 21!

LEFT, RIGHT, LEFT?   PAGE 17

1 = R, 2 = L, 3 = L, 4 = R, 5 = L, 6 = R, 7 = L, 8 = L, 9 = R, 10 = L, 11 = L, 12 = L, 13 = R, 14 = L, 15 = R, 16 = R, 17 = R, 18 = R.

QUICK SORTING   PAGE 19

All types of shape = 30.
Red shapes = 16. Green shapes =14.

Red triangles = 10. Red triangles with dot = 4; red triangles with dot and shadow = 1; red triangles with dot and no shadow = 3; red triangles without dot = 6; red triangles without dot but with shadow = 3; red triangles without dot and with no shadow = 3.
Red circles = 6. Red circles with dot = 2; red circles with dot and shadow = 1, red circles with dot but no shadow = 1; red circles without dot = 4; red circles without dot but with shadow = 2; red circles without dot and with no shadow = 2.
Green triangles = 9; green triangles with dot = 5; green triangles with dot and shadow = 4; green triangles with dot but no shadow = 1; green triangles without dot = 4; green triangles without dot but with shadow = 2; green triangles without dot and with no shadow = 2.
Green circles = 5; green circles with dot = 3; green circles with dot and shadow = 1; green circles with dot but no shadow = 2; green circles without dot = 2; green circles without dot but with shadow = 1; green circles without dot and with no shadow = 1.

To make counting easier, draw a box for each possible combination and put checks in the appropriate box as you count.

STOP THE RULER   PAGE 19

Use the scale on the right-hand edge of this page to test your reaction speed.

TURNING THE COGS   PAGE 20

A: both buckets go down. B: clockwise. C: counterclockwise.

MAKING BOXES   PAGES 20/21

1 = B, 2 = G.

SPELLING TEST   PAGE 21

Incorrectly! This word has 11 letters!

NEXT IN THE SEQUENCE   PAGE 21

On left: D. On right: C.

CHINESE WRITING   PAGE 23

MAKE A CIRCLE IN THREE MOVES   P. 23

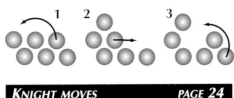

KNIGHT MOVES   PAGE 24

Move each piece in turn in a clockwise direction. After each piece has moved twice, the red knights will have changed places with the yellow knights.

MATCH THE ROTATED SHAPES   PAGE 24

First pair: B and C. Second pair: E and D. A and F do not match any of the other shapes.

ONE-SIDED PAPER   PAGE 25

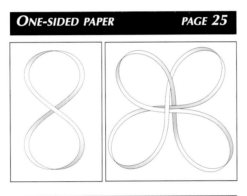

WHAT KNOT   PAGE 25

A is the slip knot.

GET UN-KNOTTED   PAGE 25

Slide the part of the other person's string that passes *under* yours up to your wrist. Insert it through the loop around your wrist, from the arm toward the hand. Pass your hand under it and pull free.

WHO IS THE TALLEST?   PAGE 27

1 = Tom. 5 = Jack. Note that in the information you are given, Tom is not taller than anyone and no one is taller than Jack.

NEXT IN THE SEQUENCE   PAGE 27

Disk A is the next in the sequence.

GUESS-THE-CARD GAME   PAGE 27

The face-down card is number 9—it is the sum of the numbers on the four cards surrounding it.

ARE YOUR WIRES CROSSED?   PAGE 27

If you try to run the pipes or cables outside the houses, the problem cannot be solved! But if you think laterally and run them underneath or through the houses, there are a number of solutions. Here is one of them.

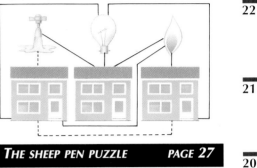

THE SHEEP PEN PUZZLE   PAGE 27

You only need two extra panels for the six new sheep. By adding an extra panel at each end of the pen, you double its size.

ISLAND MYSTERY   PAGE 29

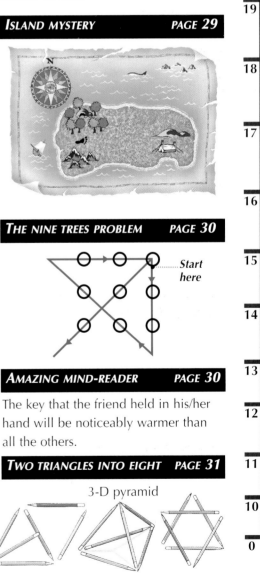

THE NINE TREES PROBLEM   PAGE 30

Start here

AMAZING MIND-READER   PAGE 30

The key that the friend held in his/her hand will be noticeably warmer than all the others.

TWO TRIANGLES INTO EIGHT   PAGE 31

3-D pyramid

THE TEN-BALL TRIANGLE   PAGE 31

Move the two outside balls on the bottom row up two rows and move the top ball down to the center bottom.

TOO SHORT TO REACH   PAGE 31

She tied the scissors to the string from the tree and let it swing. Then she held the end of the string attached to the pole, and when the other string swung toward her, she caught it and tied the two strings together.

CHICKEN-FOX-GRAIN   PAGE 32

1. The farmer takes the chicken across and leaves it. 2. He comes back and takes the fox across, but brings the chicken back with him. 3. He leaves the chicken and takes the grain across, which he leaves with the fox. 4. He comes back and gets the chicken!

COINS INTO CUPS   PAGE 33

Put five, three, and two counters into different cups. Then put the cup with three counters into the cup with two, so that it contains five counters!

TRUTHFUL AND UNTRUTHFUL TWINS P. 33

Ask either twin which road the other would say is safe; take the other road.

PUZZLE DISKS   PAGE 33

On the first move, and all subsequent odd-numbered moves, move the smallest piece in a clockwise direction. On even-numbered moves, make the only legal move not involving the smallest disk.

SEPARATING SUBSTANCES   PAGE 35

Use the magnet to separate the iron filings from the sawdust. Place the rest of the mixture in the water, and skim off the sawdust, which will float. Now put the water in a warm place until it has evaporated; this will leave the salt behind in the bowl.

THE MINIMUM OF COLORS   PAGE 35

Mathematicians have only just proved that it cannot be done!

MAKE A PAPER WING   PAGE 35

Wings give more lift if the upper surface is more curved than the lower surface.

A DISPLACEMENT GAME   PAGE 35

Weight one end of the pencil and float it upright in unsalted water. Mark the waterline on the pencil. Then float it in the two salt solutions, marking the waterline each time. The increase in the length of pencil above the water is proportional to the amount of salt in the water.

PUTTING THE COLORS. . .   PAGE 35

To mix separated colors of light with two prisms, hold one point-up and the other point-down so that they bend the light in opposite directions.

FIND THE HIDDEN OBJECTS   PAGE 36

MOVING THE BEAD, LIKE MAGIC! P.36

Push the bead up through the horizontal loop and hold it against the slit. Pull the horizontal loop through the slit from the back to the front, dragging both vertical loops with it. Pass the bead along the horizontal loop and through the two vertical loops. Return the horizontal loop to its original position and pull the bead through it until it hangs down on the other vertical loop.

CORRECT THE SUM IN NO MOVES P.37

Turn the page around by 180 degrees!

ODDS OR EVENS?   PAGE 37

It can't be done! Turning two of the same adds or subtracts an even number, leaving odd numbers odd, and even numbers even. Turning two different ones leaves the number of heads and tails the same.

TIE THE KNOT   PAGE 37

Fold your arms before holding the string! Unfolding your arms will tie the knot.

12-STRAW PROBLEM   PAGE 37

Make a cube with four square sides, a square top, and a square bottom. (You will need glue!)

SPOT THE MISTAKE   PAGE 49

COUNTING SIDES   PAGE 49

The answers are (from top down) 10, 8, 5, and 16.

COMPLETE THE PICTURE   PAGE 49

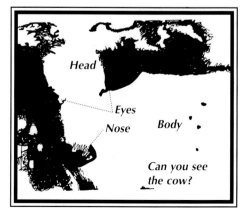

Head

Eyes

Nose   Body

Can you see the cow?

FIND THE SQUARE — PAGE 51

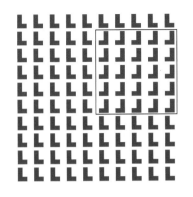

FIND THE ANIMALS — PAGE 53

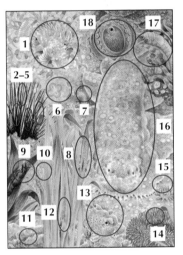

1. Sargassum fish; 2–5. Urchin shrimp fish; 6. Common jellyfish; 7. Starlet; 8. Filefish; 9. Sea hare; 10. Aesop prawn; 11. Crab; 12. Shrimp fish; 13. Stonefish; 14. Clown fish; 15. Burrowing anemone; 16. Carpet shark; 17. Clingfish; 18. Octopus.

FALSE IDENTITY — PAGE 53

Clockwise from top right: a cricket imitating a leaf; a moth that looks like bark; a moth with "eyes" on its wings; a caterpillar imitating bird droppings; a hoverfly that looks like a wasp.

COLORBLINDNESS — PAGE 55

The number in the circle is 67.

BEHIND THE SCENE — PAGE 59

The image is a horse in front of some trees.

IMPOSSIBLE PICTURE — PAGE 60

PHOTOGRAPHIC MEMORY — PAGE 68

How many deer are there in the picture? Are they the only large animals in the scene? Is the stream to the left or to the right of the trees? What time of year is it? How many geese are flying overhead? What is the landscape in the far background?

WHAT DID YOU SEE? — PAGE 69

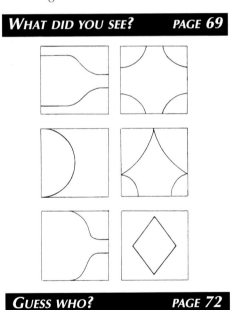

GUESS WHO? — PAGE 72

The face belongs to Abraham Lincoln, 16th President of the United States.

GUESS WHO AGAIN! — PAGE 72

It's Arnold Schwarzenegger!

A STRANGE FACE — PAGE 73

The face is upside down, and the eyes and mouth are the wrong way up.

WHAT IS IT? — PAGE 73

Snow on the tiles of a rooftop.

WHAT PLANET IS THIS? — PAGE 73

Earth, as a mirror image, with the oceans (instead of the land) shown in detail.

Glossary

Ability profile
An assessment of a person's ability to perform various tasks, often in the form of a graph or table.

Antibiotics
Chemical substances—either produced by various microorganisms such as fungi or made synthetically—that are capable of destroying bacteria.

Antiseptic
A substance that stops the growth or action of microorganisms, especially in or on living tissue.

Aptitude
A natural ability to understand or perform; another name for intelligence.

Bacteria
Single-celled microorganisms that colonize all living bodies, plants, water, soil, etc., and can cause disease.

Binocular vision
Combining the images at the backs of your retinas to form a single view of the world.

Brain function
The action of the brain that enables us to feel sensations and emotions, to think, and to remember.

Character
1. Another word for personality.
2. A letter, number, or symbol that has a well-understood meaning.

Code
A system of letters or symbols that represent other letters, symbols, or specific information. A coded message is only intelligible to a person or machine that knows the associated information; used for secret communication.

Colorblindness
Colorblindness is not being able to tell some colors apart. Red-green colorblindness is the most common form, but blue-yellow colorblindness also exists.

Color constancy
How the colors of things look the same to your eyes even though the color of the light falling on them changes.

Competition
People working toward a common objective, but trying to outdo each other.

Cone
A type of cell in the retina that turns light into an electrical message.

Cooperation
People working together in harmony to achieve a common objective.

Complementary color
The color you see as an afterimage of another color. Blue and yellow are complementary to each other; so are magenta and green.

Cryptarithmetic
Arithmetic using coded numbers.

Depth perception
Seeing the things around you as solid, and at different distances away from you.

Displacement
The weight or volume displaced by a floating object, such as a ship. Because a floating object displaces its own weight of liquid, it will float higher in a heavier liquid than in a light one.

Echolocation
Using the sound bouncing off objects to tell what they are and how far away they are.

Evolution
How living things, over many generations, come to be better adapted to their environments.

Five senses
Seeing, hearing, touch, smell, and taste. (Smell and taste are linked.)

Focus
The way in which your eyes form an image to make it clear and sharp.

Force
Any influence that makes a motionless object move, or prevents a moving object from continuing in a straight line, or causes an object to change its speed—for example to accelerate or decelerate.

Fovea
A small area of your retina where vision for detail is especially good.

Friction
The force exerted when one surface moves across another in the opposite direction.

Hand-eye coordination
Visual control of hand movements.

Imprinting
The tendency of some young birds and mammals to follow the first thing they see after they are born.

Incubator
A machine for keeping eggs warm and at a constant temperature until they hatch.

Infrared
Light with wavelengths longer than red light. It is invisible to people, but visible to some animals.

Lateral thinking
Thinking in an unconventional or unorthodox way, sometimes described as "thinking sideways."

Legal moves
A move that is allowed by the rules of a game, for example, chess.

Lens
The part of the eye behind the iris and the pupil that bends light rays to form an image. It becomes thicker or thinner to bring the image into focus, according to whether the object is near or in the distance.

Light
A form of energy that travels very fast in straight lines called rays. The energy comes in "packets" a tiny distance apart. This distance is called the wavelength. Light with a long wavelength appears red to us. Shorter wavelengths appear as orange, yellow, green, blue, indigo, and (the shortest) violet—in that order.

Lubrication
A substance such as oil that reduces friction and allows two or more objects to keep moving, even though they are in contact with each other.

Memory
A function of the brain that enables us to remember past experiences. How the brain stores memories is not yet understood.

Optical illusion
A picture or object that plays tricks on your eyes, causing you to see something that is not really there, or something different from what really is there.

Personality
The sum total of our likes, interests, abilities, and mental characteristics. Personality is what makes each individual unique.

Perspective
The way that the layout of a real scene is expressed in the shape of a picture or image.

Primary color
One of three colors that can be mixed in different combinations to produce other colors. Red, blue, and green are the primary colors of light; red, blue, and yellow are the primary colors of pigments. Mixing colored light is different from mixing pigments because the color of the pigment depends on the wavelengths of light absorbed by the pigment. If you mix red, blue, and green paints you get dark gray, because the mixture absorbs all wavelengths to almost the same degree. But if you add red, green, and blue light in the right proportions, you get white light. When two primary colors overlap, they produce a secondary color—for example, red and green make yellow.

Programmed
Instructed to respond in a particular way. The term is usually applied to a computer that has been given instructions in a coded form that it can read.

Pupil
A circular opening just in front of the lens, which allows light into your eye.

Radiant heat
Sending out heat (electromagnetic waves) by radiation. X-rays, light, radiant heat, microwaves, and radio waves are all electromagnetic waves of progressively longer wavelengths.

Retina
The layer of light-sensitive cells that covers the back of your eye.

Rod
A type of cell in the retina that turns light into an electrical message and can work in dim light.

Scientist
A person who uses the scientific methods of observing, experimenting, developing theories, and then testing the theories to arrive at a conclusion.

Sensation
An impression perceived through one of the five main senses: sight, sound, touch, smell, and taste.

Spectrum
The series of colors you see as light changes wavelength. The full spectrum is made up of red, orange, yellow, green, blue, indigo, and violet.

Topology
The study of the shapes of things.

Trifoiler
A sailboard with two wings (foils) in the water parallel to the main board, which lift it as it speeds up. This reduces resistance and helps it go faster.

Ultraviolet
Light with wavelengths shorter than violet light. It is invisible to people, but visible to some animals.

Virtual reality
A way of making television pictures change as you move around, in the same way as if you moved through a real scene.

Visualization
Creating a "picture in your head" of an imaginary scene or object.

Vocation
A desire to follow a particular occupation such as teaching or medicine, or to devote one's life to a religious calling.

Wavelength
The tiny distance between two waves of energy in a ray of light. Wavelength determines color: red has the longest wavelength, and violet has the shortest, with other colors in between.

Zoologist
A scientist who studies the science and characteristics of animals.

Index

Numbers in *italics* refer to captions.